READING AND UNDERSTANDING THE MYSTERIES OF

TAROT

READING AND UNDERSTANDING THE MYSTERIES OF

TAROT

LEARN HOW TO DISCOVER AND EXPLAIN YOUR DESTINY
BY UNLOCKING THE FASCINATING SECRETS OF THE CARDS

STACI MENDOZA
AND DAVID BOURNE

LORENZ BOOKS

This edition is published by Lorenz Books
an imprint of Anness Publishing Ltd
Hermes House
88–89 Blackfriars Road, London SE1 8HA
tel. 020 7401 2077; fax 020 7633 9499

www.lorenzbooks.com; www.annesspublishing.com

If you like the images in this book and would like to
investigate using them for publishing, promotions or
advertising, please visit our website
www.practicalpictures.com for more information.

UK distributor: Book Trade Services; tel. 0116 2759086;
fax 0116 2759090; uksales@booktradeservices.com;
exportsales@booktradeservices.com

North American distributor: National Book Network;
tel. 301 459 3366; fax 301 429 5746;
www.nbnbooks.com

Australian distributor: Pan Macmillan Australia;
tel. 1300 135 113; fax 1300 135 103;
customer.service@macmillan.com.au

New Zealand distributor: David Bateman Ltd;
tel. (09) 415 7664; fax (09) 415 8892

Publisher: Joanna Lorenz
Project Editor: Amy Christian
Editorial Reader: Lauren Taylor
Photography: John Freeman and Michelle Garrett
Designer: Design Principals
Production Controller: Mai-Ling Collyer
Indexer: Ann Barrett

© Anness Publishing Ltd 2011

A CIP catalogue record for this book is available from
the British Library.

This is an enlarged and expanded edition of
New Life Library: Tarot

ETHICAL TRADING POLICY
At Anness Publishing we believe that business should be
conducted in an ethical and ecologically sustainable way,
with respect for the environment and a proper regard to
the replacement of the natural resources we employ.

As a publisher, we use a lot of wood pulp in high-quality
paper for printing, and that wood commonly comes from
spruce trees. We are therefore currently growing more than
750,000 trees in three Scottish forest plantations:
Berrymoss (130 hectares/320 acres), West Touxhill
(125 hectares/305 acres) and Deveron Forest
(75 hectares/185 acres). The forests we manage contain
more than 3.5 times the number of trees employed each
year in making paper for the books we manufacture.

Because of this ongoing ecological investment programme,
you, as our customer, can have the pleasure and reassurance
of knowing that a tree is being cultivated on your behalf to
naturally replace the materials used to make the book you
are holding.

Our forestry programme is run in accordance with the
UK Woodland Assurance Scheme (UKWAS) and will be
certified by the internationally recognized Forest
Stewardship Council (FSC). The FSC is a non-government
organization dedicated to promoting responsible
management of the world's forests. Certification ensures
forests are managed in an environmentally sustainable and
socially responsible way. For further information about
this scheme, go to www.annesspublishing.com/trees.

PUBLISHER'S NOTE
Although the advice and information in this book are
believed to be accurate and true at the time of going to
press, neither the authors nor the publisher can accept any
legal responsibility or liability for any errors or omissions
that may have been made nor for any inaccuracies nor for
any loss, harm or injury that comes about from following
instructions or advice in this book.

CONTENTS

Introduction

For hundreds of years, the Tarot has been a source of mystery and fascination, intriguing us with its compelling and enigmatic pictures and symbols. No one really knows where the Tarot originated, or how or why it may work. One thing seems certain though: if we can 'tune in' with the images presented to us on the cards, then we can gain access to a deeper understanding of ourselves and the people and events involved in our lives.

The Tarot deck as we know it is composed of 78 cards, which divide into two clear parts: the 22 cards of the Major Arcana and the 56 cards of the Minor Arcana.

The Minor Arcana is further sub-divided into four suits: Swords, Wands, Pentacles and Cups. The Minor Arcana closely parallels a normal pack of 52 playing cards with its suits of Clubs, Spades, Hearts and Diamonds.

The Major Arcana reflects the major turning points in our lives: our commitments, triumphs and tragedies, whilst the cards of the Minor Arcana deal with the more day-to-day aspects of life. Taken together, they constitute a guidebook to the incidents and issues that we have to handle in our lives, from the past, the present and looking to the future.

This book is designed to be a practical reference guide to help you become acquainted with this ancient system of divination. It gives concise key background information to the Tarot, followed by general definitions for each of the cards. Finally, it suggests different Tarot spreads and ways in which you can put this advice into practice by giving actual Tarot readings for yourself, your friends and family.

Although this book contains general guidelines about what the cards mean, the ultimate aim is for you to develop your own intuitive skills using the Tarot and to arrive at your own conclusions. In the end, each reader and their interpretation is as unique as a set of finger-prints. The Tarot has the potential to be endlessly original and fresh, and perhaps this is why it is still just as popular today as it was hundreds of years ago.

Left: As you read, you will develop an understanding of the different meanings behind the cards in a Tarot deck.

Choosing a Tarot deck

A Tarot deck is as unique as the person reading it. Today, a wide range of Tarot decks are available in many different styles and genres. There are very modern decks with abstract, graphic designs through to more traditionally themed decks inspired by such things as fairies, dragons and other mythological creatures. There are some decks based entirely around ancient cultures such as the Celts, Egyptians or Vikings and of course there are the great classical decks, some of which date back hundreds of years.

Some decks are very bright, utilizing vivid primary colours, while some are quite pastel and muted in their shades. Some decks are painted or drawn by artists and some are composed entirely of images or photographs digitally generated on a computer.

Whatever the design, for the purposes of a Tarot reading a full 78-card Tarot deck will be needed. This deck can be illustrated with whatever you are drawn to. It is important that the colours and designs of the Tarot deck appeal to the individual that will be using them, but the 78 independent classical meanings of the cards will remain the same.

For the beginner new to Tarot it is wise to choose a deck which has all 78 cards clearly and entirely illustrated. The best decks for the beginner will have a picture illustrating the whole meaning, for example The Seven of Swords card should show an illustration of the seven swords. The more pictorially based the images are, the easier it will be for the user to remember the meanings.

Above: As a beginner, choose a Tarot deck with simple illustrations that appeal to you on a personal level.

As they become more proficient, beginners may move on to using a more advanced deck where the imagery is more abstract and less pictorially structured. This will help to push the reader's psychic abilities further because they cannot depend on pictorial prompts for the definitions of the cards.

The most important thing to remember is that whatever the type of Tarot deck that is chosen, at the end of the day it is only a tool – albeit a useful one – that is used in communication with ourselves and with others.

Using the Tarot for oneself

The Tarot is an excellent tool for many self-help purposes. When the 78 individual representations in the Tarot are studied it can help with picture memory recognition. The process of visual recall is vital while using the Tarot cards during a reading, as the reader must rely on their own memory for the relevant definitions.

As it is such a fascinating subject, learning about Tarot helps to stimulate the mind into different thinking processes, on both a creative and visual level. This often occurs when a person begins to study something new and exciting for the first time.

At some stage in life, each of the 78 definitions of the Tarot cards can be personally related to an individual's own experience or the experiences of those closely associated with them. The whole process of learning to use the Tarot allows the individual to become more introspective and hopefully to develop a deeper and more meaningful understanding of themselves.

The Tarot can be an excellent tool when used within the practice of meditation. This is the case for both the novice and the more experienced reader. For example, on a daily basis an individual could randomly select a card, look at the image for a few moments, taking in all its details, and consider its definition. Once the person feels they have done this for a suitable time, so as to capture the card's image, they could meditate by finding a comfortable place to sit, closing their eyes and visualizing the image that they have studied within their mind's eye. Meditation is a personal experience and practice for us all, so if you have your own preferred techniques that work for you, try and incorporate the Tarot into your meditation ritual in some way.

The process of meditation, no matter which technique is used, helps a person to build a visual relationship with each of the individual 78 Tarot cards and their definitions. This type of visually close relationship comes into its own when several cards are laid out in a Tarot spread for interpreting. If the reader has spent time meditating and quietly familiarizing themselves with the cards, each image in the spread will be easily recognizable in a reading. This makes the interpretation of the Tarot cards much easier.

Above: When using the Tarot for self-help, meditation can be an effective way of getting to know the Tarot deck.

Using the Tarot for others

Almost everyone who wants to learn about the Tarot is interested in it primarily as a tool for divination. The Tarot is often revered, and sometimes feared, because of the mystery surrounding its creation and historical use.

The Tarot is a pictorially-based tool for communicating with others. While other media such as the theatre or film communicate with a wider audience on a broader level, the Tarot is an intimate form of communication which is truly a one-to-one experience. This intimacy allows for deeper and more personal issues to be discussed and expressed without an audience.

The place in which a Tarot reading is given to another person needs careful consideration. The setting needs to be away from the hustle and bustle of the world outside, ideally in a quiet and calm area with soft lighting. Any background noise or music playing should be subtle and not invasive enough to intrude on the reading. This will allow for a calm and sensitive approach to the variety of possible topics, and sometimes deeply personal issues, that could be raised.

The room that the reading is conducted in must be comfortable and welcoming, and the décor must be pleasing to the eye with no distractions to interfere with the concentration of the person you are reading for or your own. Make sure that the person you are reading for is at ease, and try to put to rest any anxieties they

Above: When giving a Tarot reading, the setting is very important. It should be calm, quiet and relaxing.

have about the process of the reading beforehand. Be clear and precise with your answers to any questions from the person you are reading for, before, during or after the reading. Make sure that any questions you have in relation to the reading are understandable and not too leading, for it is your job in this process to be the counselling ear, the good friend that offers sound advice.

Finally, it is important to remember that the study and practice of Tarot is above all to be enjoyed. Readings should not be rushed or too prying. Any insights gained need to be communicated in a humane and kindly manner. The reader needs to be constructive, sensitive and unbiased in giving advice and, most importantly, any information and issues discussed with another should always stay strictly confidential.

The origins of Tarot

Although the Tarot is one of the best-known forms of divination, its precise origins remain shrouded in mystery. The cards have existed in the form that we now know them for 200 years. Various theories have been put forward by esoteric scholars about their exact origins, some suggesting the cards are from ancient Egypt, others that they see strong links with Hebrew mysticism. However, the first real evidence of the Tarot's existence dates back to Renaissance Italy.

In the mid-15th century, the Duchy of Milan was ruled over by the Visconti family – a name that has remained synonymous with the cards. The Viscontis commissioned Bonifacio Bembo to paint a set of 78 unnamed and unnumbered

Left: Filippo Maria Visconti, 1392–1447, a member of the wealthy family that commissioned the first Tarot deck.

cards that depicted religious allegories, social conditions and ideas of the time. They were painted to celebrate a marriage between the Sforza and Visconti families, and formed the deck for an Italian gambling game called 'Tarocchi'. It is uncertain whether the cards had any esoteric significance at the time or if they were devised only for game-playing.

In the late 18th century we find the Tarot cards recorded as being used as a divinatory tool. Between 1773–82, the Frenchman Antoine Court de Gébelin published an eight-volume work called *Le Monde Primitif*. Here he speculated on the origins of the Tarot (which was the French name for Tarocchi), and offered the view that the cards originated in ancient Egypt and used as a 'book' of magical wisdom. At the time of de Gébelin, there was considerable interest in ancient Egypt, and many people believed that Egyptian hieroglyphs were magical symbols concealing lost knowledge of the past. The ground was therefore fertile for de Gébelin's theory, which gained credence with many people.

Following in the footsteps of de Gébelin came Tarot students, each one of whom added to the links and analogies that make the current Tarot.

Left: Portrait of Maria Sforza *by Bonifacio Bembo (1447–78). The original Tarot deck is named after the Sforza family.*

This development reached its height in the 19th and early 20th centuries. In 1854, the book *Transcendental Magic* was published in France. Its author was Alphonse Louis Constance, originally a deacon in the Catholic church, but better known by his Hebrew pen-name, Eliphas Lévi. He linked each of the 22 cards of the Major Arcana with one of the 22 letters from the Hebrew alphabet. Lévi was the first person to insist on a link between the Kabbalah, a Jewish mystic tradition with its own system of esoteric thought, and the Tarot, saying that one could not be understood without the other.

It was Lévi's system, still in use by many French occultists today, that provided a stepping stone for one of the most well-known Western magical orders to begin their work: the secret Order of the Golden Dawn, founded c.1886. Its members took up the Tarot, and began developments that would lead to new schools of thought. These changes were largely brought about by the work of two of its members: Arthur Edward Waite and Aleister Crowley.

In 1909, Waite commissioned the American artist Pamela Coleman-Smith to paint a set of images for his 'rectified' Tarot. This deck of cards, known as the Rider-Waite Tarot (Rider was the London company that published them), became one of the most influential Tarot decks of the 20th century. It is used all over the world today. It was the first deck to depart from tradition by using pictures for the numbered suits of the Minor Arcana. Crowley had a reputation as an actor, magician and womanizer, but he was also a serious esoteric scholar and Kabbalist. In the early

Above: King of Woods 1941, *watercolour by Lady Frieda Harris, from the Tarot pack designed by Aleister Crowley.*

20th century, he decided to create his own deck and asked Lady Frieda Harris to paint it. The Thoth Tarot was published in 1969, but neither Crowley nor Harris lived to see it. Crowley modernized the existing deck by re-positioning The Fool, the unnumbered Major Arcana card, at the start of his Tarot deck, and transposed the Justice and Strength cards. Crowley also included a system of astrological connections with each of the Major cards, thus departing from the traditional French system.

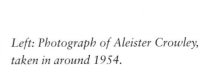

Left: Photograph of Aleister Crowley, taken in around 1954.

The aspects of Tarot

The Tarot is designed to relate, pictorially, to what we are feeling inside. It reflects our psychological and emotional state as well as showing us the people and events involved in our lives. The aim is to use the images on the cards as a springboard, allowing their own intuitive meaning to come through. However, the general guidelines on the following pages may be applied.

The symbolism and meanings of the Tarot, as presented in this book, are taken from a popular and traditional point of view. They represent an overview of the basic imagery that has been present in many forms in the cards during their history.

Today there are hundreds of Tarot decks available, each with their own vision and ideas about the Tarot. However, although a lot of decks will look very different to the descriptions in this book, in most cases these descriptions will remain valid. When you buy a new pack, all the cards will come in

Above: Vanitas c.1634, *by Antonio Pereda y Salgado. The general meanings behind the Tarot cards have a long history.*

numerical and sequential order. To learn each card's definition, it is probably useful to follow this order. Once the definitions have been mastered, however, there is no need to keep the cards in any particular order. When reading the cards for yourself or others, some people like to distinguish between Upright and Reversed directions.

UPRIGHT
This refers to the card when it is facing pictorially upright when it is laid out in a Tarot spread right-side up. It reflects the meaning of the card in its purest form.

REVERSED
This direction refers to the card when it is facing upside-down in a spread. The reversed direction can indicate a subtle change or significantly alter the meaning of the card.

ACES

The Ace is the crowning card in any deck. Mathematically valued as either one or eleven, it is usually a matter of personal choice as to which way you want it to add up. It can be used to win in card-playing games due to its mathematical duality. This theme of winning or victory is also present in the Tarot, and Aces are usually seen as extremely positive cards and as the keystones of the Minor Arcana.

The Aces contain the powerful energy of the entire suit that they represent; the absolute truth of that particular element, whether it is fire, water, air or earth. They are of great help when approaching any new or difficult situation. The Ace cards are from the suits of Swords, Wands, Pentacles and Cups. The Major Arcana has no Ace card but the unnumbered Fool takes up its place in this grouping.

EIGHTS

The Eights have a special role and are particularly important in a reading. This is because the figure eight (8) relates to the symbol of infinity, the never-ending cycle of life in which our lives spiral, always constant yet always changing. Any of the Eights will therefore highlight changes in our lives and the sense of moving forward. These cards are the eighth Major Arcana card, Strength or Justice (depending on the pack), and the Eights in the suits of Swords, Wands, Pentacles and Cups.

COMBINATIONS OF MULTIPLES

Aces: One Ace signifies a good omen. Multiple Aces signify an even better omen.
Twos: One Two signifies a rut or a standstill. Two Twos indicate balance. Three or more Twos signify a great imbalance.

Threes: In any quantity Threes indicate activity and movement. The more Threes, the greater the activity and movement.

Fours: In any quantity Fours indicate stability and strength.

Fives: In any quantity Fives indicate problems. The greater the number of Fives the greater the problems.

Sixes: One Six in a spread signifies a good omen. Two or more appearing indicate the feeling of being overburdened.

Sevens: Any amount of Sevens indicates good luck, a renewal of energies.

Eights: Signify the continuum of time and motion, within a Tarot spread they act as a stepping point from one situation to another.

Nines: In any quantity in a spread Nines indicate forthcoming problems.

Tens: In any quantity Tens indicate energy and vitality, also the coming of positive changes.

Pages: In any quantity Pages indicate harmony and communication.

Knights: Indicate a seeking tendency and any more than one Knight indicates chaos.

Queens: Any more than two Queens indicates excessive emotional influences in a situation.

Kings: More than two Kings indicates too much power or pressure being applied to a situation.

Above: In any Tarot deck the four Aces are the most important cards in the Minor Arcana.

Astrology in the Tarot

The Planetary Chart and the Astrology Chart here relate to the planetary and astrological similes found and attributed to the existing 78-card Tarot deck. Generally the attributes and links of the elements, planets and signs have remained the same over a long period of time. Astrology reflects very harmoniously with and within the Tarot, as it, like the cards, deals with people and their life issues. These charts should be used as part of a Tarot reading. By looking up the Tarot cards in the charts, the reader can gain further information that will help them to pinpoint a person's star sign, character attributes, possible appearance and behaviour patterns within the confines of a Tarot spread. Within the astrological chart notice that there is one Major Arcana and one Minor Arcana per star sign. This gives a better all round insight into the person represented in the Tarot spread.

PLANETARY CHART

ELEMENT	PLANET	TAROT CARD
Air Prefers intellectual pursuits. Very literal, needs facts. Drawn to mental challenges. A powerful sense of self.	Uranus Creative thought. Intuition. Non-conformity. Freedom.	The Fool New beginnings and ventures. Taking on change for the experience of change.
	Mercury Inquisitiveness. Mental Agility. Intellect. Curiosity.	The Magician Getting plans and all aspects of life organized
Water Sensual and sensitive. Artistic and intuitively inclined. Very attractive to look at. Likes culture and romance.	The Moon Emotions. Feelings. Nurturing. Reflection.	The High Priestess Listening to gut feelings. Trusting inside intuition. Looking behind the scenes for the truth.
	Neptune Artistic inspiration. Mystical thought. Enlightenment. Illusion.	The Hanged Man Life at a standstill. Time to reflect on past decisions in order to bring about change.
Earth Good problem-solver. Well balanced and purposeful. Possessing inherent wisdom with a need to be useful.	Venus Feeling welcomed. Feminine instincts. Sensuality. Laws of attraction. Romance.	The Empress Fertility and warmth. Good house atmosphere.
	Saturn Discipline. Order. Karmic issues. Control over destiny.	The World Indicates success in most areas of life. Contentment
Fire Strong basic instincts. Quick in temper and quick to cool down. Physically active and sporty.	Jupiter Good fortune. Risk taking. Purpose. Expansion.	The Wheel of Fortune Fate taking a strong hand in life. New direction.
	The Sun Energy. Growth. Strength. Vitality.	The Sun Potential and growth. Progression. Expansion.
	Pluto Freedom of movement. Power. Obsession. Regeneration. Abuse.	The Judgement A rut is ending. Time to break free. No restrictions.
	Mars Lust. Skilfulness. Self-preservation.	The Tower Unforeseen disruptions. Chaos and disagreement.

ASTROLOGY CHART

ELEMENT	SIGN	TAROT CARDS	
Air Prefers intellectual pursuits. Very literal and needs facts. Drawn to mental challenges. A powerful sense of self.	Aquarius Vision. Originality. Individuality. Independence.	The Star Wishes and dreams coming true.	King of Swords Person of great fortitude and loyalty.
	Gemini Versatility. Flexibility. Quickness of Mind. Dexterity.	The Lovers Charismatic relationship with spontaneity.	Knight of Swords Person feeling energetic and ready for action.
	Libra Fairness. Vision. Idealism. Charm.	Justice Balance and fairness being carried out.	Queen of Swords Person of great fortitude and loyalty.
Water Sensual and sensitive. Artistic and intuitively inclined. Very attractive to look at. Likes culture and romance.	Pisces Perception. Creativity. Awareness. Spirituality.	The Moon Deceptive forces at play. Creative thought patterns.	Knight of Cups Person seeking love and affirmation.
	Cancer Imagination. Insight. Tenacity. Tenderness.	The Chariot Triumph or victory which is hard won.	Queen of Cups Person of great emotional sensitivity.
	Scorpio Discipline. Tenderness. Magnetism. Dedication.	Death New era. New outlook. Regeneration. Rebirth.	King of Cups Person of great social skill, with humour.
Earth Good problem solver. Well-balanced and purposeful. Possessing inherent wisdom with a need to be useful.	Taurus Logic. Sensuality. Industry. Determination.	The Hierophant Recognized state and church. Professional knowledge.	Knight of Pentacles Person with great ambition.
	Virgo Discernment. Courtesy. Servitude. Practicality.	The Hermit Solitude and self-analysis. Contemplation	King of Pentacles Person handling responsibility and love together well.
	Capricorn Wisdom. Ambition. Generosity. Dependability.	The Devil Passion. Energy. Desire.	Queen of Pentacles Person of great warmth and kindness.
Fire Strong basic instincts. Quick in temper and quick to cool down. Physically active and sporty.	Aries Courage. Affability. Enterprise. Heartiness.	The Emperor Establishment and steadiness.	Queen of Wands Person of drama and intrigue.
	Leo Nobility. Power. Warmth. Loyalty.	Strength Gentle patience and insight.	King of Wands Person of loving nature and freedom
	Sagittarius Reason. Generosity. Cheerfulness. Chivalry.	Temperance Thinking before action. Caution.	Knight of Wands Person soul-searching, looking for the answers to life.

The Major Arcana

There are 21 numbered cards in the Major Arcana and one unnumbered card – The Fool – which brings the group's total to 22 cards in all. The Major Arcana cards reflect major turning points in life. They represent the states which may affect all of us at some time in our lives, like birth, love, marriage and death. As the Major Arcana cards are so significant in their actions and how they affect us, they will always take special precedence in a Tarot spread, reflecting the more important and challenging points in our lives. Around all this major moving and shaking, there is the card of The Fool; a childlike figure that transiently moves through the world of the Major Arcana and gives it its 22nd card. Looking at the group of cards as a whole, the Major Arcana can be broken down into three distinct groups consisting of seven cards in each.

Right: The meanings behind the cards of the Major Arcana are relevant to major events in our lives.

THE THREE REALMS

The first group of seven cards – The Magician, The High Priestess, The Empress, The Emperor, The Hierophant, The Lovers and The Chariot – deal with what is termed as The Realm of the Material World. These are issues which are connected to commitment through society's laws, such as marriage, success, higher education and the family.

The second group of seven cards – Justice, The Hermit, The Wheel of Fortune, Strength, The Hanged Man, Death and Temperance – deal with The Realms of the Intuitive World. These are issues that are connected to the individual rather than society as whole.

The third and most significant group of seven cards – The Devil, The Tower, The Star, The Moon, The Sun, Judgment and The World – deal with The Realm of the Changing Issues. These are issues which shape or redirect a person's life direction or circumstances, they represent those universal laws

Right: There are 21 numbered cards and one unnumbered card – The Fool – that make up the Major Arcana.

and concerns that have the power to bring about the kind of circumstances and events that can alter the course of our lives.

THE COURT CARDS

Within the Major Arcana is the first set of High Court cards. These are The High Priestess, who is adviser to the Empress (or Queen) and Emperor (or King) in supernatural matters, and The Hierophant, who is the Empress and Emperor's legal and spiritual adviser. There are four other Court card groups within the Tarot deck and they can be found amongst the Swords, Wands, Pentacles and Cups which are located in the Minor Arcana.

ASTROLOGY AND TAROT

In addition to the High Court cards and the three groups of seven which divide the Major Arcana, astrology also has a role in this part of the Tarot deck. The Sun, the Moon, the twelve signs of the zodiac and the planets of our solar system are all reflected within the cards of the Major Arcana, while the four suits of the Minor Arcana have astrological associations with the four classical elements of astrology: Earth, Air, Fire and Water. (See the Planetary Chart and Astrology Chart for more detail.)

THE FOOL

The only oddity of the Major Arcana is The Fool, whose number is zero. In medieval times, The Fool held a special place in society. For many people, this character was an innocent, in contact with the gods, and was able to say and do more or less anything he liked. It is this idea that

influenced the card imagery of The Fool when the Tarot was developed, and thus The Fool jumped into the Major Arcana in its own unique and individual way.

Much mystery surrounds The Fool and the fact that it does not have a number. One theory is that this stems from the early superstitious belief that odd numbers were associated with bad omens while even numbers were associated with good omens. (Superstition around the number thirteen still exists today.) The Fool was perhaps left unnumbered to make it neutral, to remove any question of it being a good or bad omen. Zero is traditionally associated with new beginnings, conception, a start and a stepping stone from the divine spark of life into physical living.

The Fool does not fit into any of the three sections of seven cards in the Major Arcana and so it can be placed either at the beginning or at the end of the Major group, in a similar way to the Aces of the Minor Suits. This decision is traditionally left to the individual to decide for themselves, but for the purposes of this book and for learning the Major Arcana definitions, The Fool has been placed at the beginning.

0 The Fool

Traditionally, the fool is represented as a young, androgynous figure with a look of wonder in his eyes. He is sometimes pictured sniffing a beautiful rose so intently that he does not notice he is just about to step over a dangerous cliff. The figure often carries a staff with a bag attached to it, whilst at his heels a small animal snaps, almost as if it is trying to force the character over the ledge. The Fool is seen as an adventurous card and the feeling of change is often associated with it.

UPRIGHT

This card denotes a fresh start and a sense of spontaneity. New experiences and directions are occurring so accept the process of change. You will be taking a risk or an unknown step forwards, but the joy and excitement is in the experience of change and not in the end result.

REVERSED

A foolish individual who doesn't think before venturing out, hence frequently making considerable mistakes. It would be better to stop and take time to evaluate matters before forging ahead. This could also indicate a childish view of life and not accepting responsibilities.

THE REALM OF THE MATERIAL WORLD

The seven cards in the first group of the Major Arcana deal with situations that are connected to commitment through society's laws, such as marriage, success, higher education and the family.

1 The Magician

A man stands behind a table. His left hand is raised, and in it he holds a wand. Before him on the table lies a sword, a cup, a wand and a pentacle (or coin). Above his head (or in the shape of his hat) there is an infinity symbol, and sometimes flowers and other greenery surround him.

UPRIGHT

This is a preparation card, warning you that you should try to bring all the elements of your life together: love, emotions, action, finances and morality. This is in preparation for changes ahead so that you can handle situations correctly.

REVERSED

This card indicates an individual who generally conducts themselves with great presence and perfectionism, and who appears to always have it "together". A person who handles chaotic situations and circumstances effortlessly and with great ease.

II The High Priestess

The High Priestess is represented by a woman. She is dressed in long draping robes, and sits on a chair between two pillars. The pillar on the left is often dark whilst the one on the right is light. Between them hangs a veil behind which can be seen a flowing stream. The woman holds a book, which sometimes has the word "TARO" written on it, and she often wears the symbol of the crescent moon.

UPRIGHT

This cards shows that you should try to trust in your own intuition. Do not take things at face value but take the time to look behind the scenes. Look for the answers to your questions from within your own heart. Use logic less to come to the right conclusion.

REVERSED

Everything is now out in the open; nothing is hidden from you and all the facts of the matter are obvious to see. When reversed, this card tells you that you should now be able to make your decision, and find the answers to your questions with confidence, using both your powers of intuition and your logic.

III The Empress

The Empress is represented by a voluptuous woman – often with fair hair, clothed in a long flowing dress and smiling serenely. She wears a crown and in her left hand she holds a sceptre with a globe on the end of it. In her other hand she has a protective shield with the symbol of an eagle on it. She is normally depicted seated in natural surroundings and, sometimes, behind her a stream flows. For women, she represents security and motherhood.

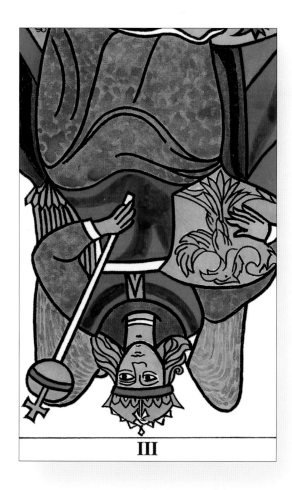

UPRIGHT

This is the key card to indicate fertility or pregnancy. If it comes up for a man or a woman outside child-bearing years, its meaning is one of domestic bliss, the feeling that "all is well in your home". The Empress represents a woman who has the ability to make people feel welcomed and loved in her own home.

REVERSED

An earthy woman whose main enjoyment in life is to care for others. A woman who by her own nature could not turn a soul away when they are in need. When reversed, the Empress can also mean disharmony in the home due to outside influences, such as the visit of a difficult relative or a disruptive child.

IV The Emperor

The Emperor is represented by an older man sitting on a throne. He often holds a sceptre in one hand and in the other an imperial orb with a cross on it, which is traditionally a sign of authority. Sometimes he has a large eagle on his hat, or has a shield decorated with the image of an eagle, another symbol of his power. He signifies a male influence, confidence and worldly power, and a person well capable of using authority.

UPRIGHT

This card deals with any form of established organization, such as banks, schools, governmental offices or established companies. It could also mean that you are trying to establish a company or organization of your own.

REVERSED

Disorganization and conflict with established organizations. Perhaps taking for granted an established reputation or position of authority, leading to complacency. It is now time to take action and point out where there are problems.

V | The Hierophant

Also known as "The High Priest", this figure is the male counterpart of the High Priestess. Like her, he also sits between two pillars but his are both the same colour. He is dressed in the robes of a churchman and wears a triple papal crown. He offers a benediction with his right hand and in his left hand he holds a sceptre with a cross on the top. Before him kneel two supplicants and sometimes, at his feet, are two keys. He represents professional advice, teaching and learning.

UPRIGHT

This card shows the need to seek professional advice from people such as doctors, lawyers and financial advisers. Alternatively, any ritualistic service that is performed under the eyes and jurisdiction of the Church, such as marriage, christenings, or divorce.

REVERSED

This shows a person who lives their life according to society's rules; a follower, usually quite an academic person, such as an accountant, lawyer or doctor. Usually this card will also represent a stable and successful individual.

VI The Lovers

A young man stands at a crossroads that branches off to the right and left. On each path a woman waits. The fair-haired woman stands on the right and the dark-haired on the left. Above the man flies Cupid or an angel, offering him the choice of either of these two paths. This card usually indicates love or possibly the beginning of a romance.

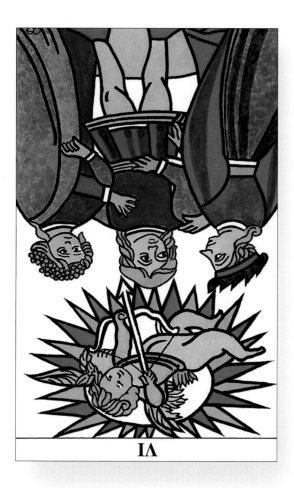

UPRIGHT

Instant chemistry between two people. An intimate relationship formed by a chance meeting, in which fate plays a part, such as missing your train by seconds, but taking the next one and meeting "Mr-" or "Ms Right".

REVERSED

When reversed, this card represents an individual who challenges society's rules regarding gender roles. This includes people who do not easily fall into a particular stereotype.

VII The Chariot

A strong-looking figure rides in a chariot pulled by two sphinxes or perhaps horses. In many decks the sphinx, or horse, on the left is light and the one on the right is dark, signifying good and evil. In the man's right hand there is a wand or sceptre. The canopy of the chariot is sometimes decorated in stars.

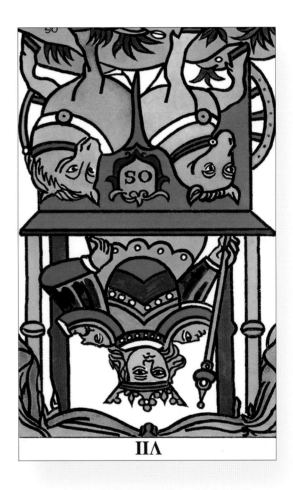

UPRIGHT

A triumphant victory in life, which was quite a challenge to win. Even though you may be facing many obstacles, there is the feeling that what you are doing is the right thing.

REVERSED

At this time, it would be unwise to apply any more pressure to the situation concerned. If you do, you risk pushing people or circumstances over the limit and failing.

THE REALM OF THE INTUITIVE MIND

The second group of seven Major Arcana cards focuses more on the individual than on society and worldly concerns. Decisions are based more on how you feel rather than on what you think.

VIII Justice

SIGN OF LIBRA

A woman sits on a throne. In her left hand she holds a set of scales and in her other a great double-edged sword. She is sometimes blindfolded. This card indicates fairness and balance. In some Tarot decks Justice is number 11 and Strength is number 8.

UPRIGHT

Justice will now be served. This is a very favourable card in a karmic sense, because whatever the outcome of a particular circumstance, it will be a fair one.

REVERSED

An injustice will take place. The outcome of a particular circumstance will be unfair. This card can also indicate bias and imbalance.

IX The Hermit

PLANET OF
JUPITER

An old man stands at the top of a high mountain. He wears the dark robes of a monk and in one hand he holds a staff. In his other hand is a lantern which he shines before him. The light from the lantern emits rays of light that resemble the beams of a star.

UPRIGHT

You need to take time for yourself to regain energy and gather your thoughts. Take refuge in your own company and do the things that will make you happy.

REVERSED

An individual who finds it difficult to take advice, and at times suffers for their pride. Consider the advice of others at this time because they have your best interests at heart.

X The Wheel of Fortune

PLANET OF
JUPITER

There is a wheel with Fortune in the middle. Sometimes the letters TARO are written upon the wheel in the positions of north, south, east and west, as if the wheel were a compass. Sometimes figures climb up the outside of the wheel. In this deck at the top of the wheel on a platform is a sphinx, in other decks it is often a man with ass's ears. This card indicates destiny and fate.

UPRIGHT

Fate will now take a strong hand in life and redirect the path that you are on. Sometimes this change can be really positive, such as an award for merit, or it can be something negative, such as a job redundancy. Either way the matter is beyond your control, but the path taken after this redirection is in your own hands. Stay adaptable and take advantage of chance events.

REVERSED

Although you may have been finding that life has been a little difficult of late and you may have experienced a run of bad luck, this card indicates that things are changing and your life will soon be taking a turn for the better. Everything is on the way up again, and now it is time to herald and enjoy the positive changes that are coming in your direction.

XI Strength

The Strength or Fortitude card in most decks is represented by a young man or woman controlling a lion in some manner. In this deck, a woman has her hands clasped around the lion's open mouth. This card indicates moral strength, self-discipline and courage. In some decks Strength is number 8 and Justice is number 11.

UPRIGHT

This card indicates that there is no need for you to worry, or to lose sight of your goals. Even if the road that you find yourself on at the moment is a difficult one, you will be sure to get there in the end. Strength shows you that you should try to be patient and persevere. Try to have more confidence in yourself and your own abilities.

REVERSED

When it is reversed, the Strength card shows that you may be feeling a need to seek some reassurance from a trusted source in order to help you get back on track at this difficult time in your life. It is now the right time for you to begin to re-evaluate your position and work out exactly where you are going, or where you want to go.

XII The Hanged Man

A young man hangs from a tree by his left leg. His right leg is folded behind the left, making a shape which resembles the number four. His arms are folded behind his back. The man's face does not look tortured but in fact is quite serene.

UPRIGHT

Life is at a standstill or in a rut. Although things may not be to your liking, it is not as bad as you think. It is best to take life patiently at the moment and bide your time until you see that the timing is right to make the necessary changes and improvements to your situation.

REVERSED

This card represents a great contentment in life. You are feeling very happy with your present situation and the position in which you find yourself. Things are going so well for you at the moment that you feel you are almost blissful.

XIII Death

A skeletal figure wields a bow or large scythe. The ground is cracked and in some decks he is walking through a field of bones and cutting off the heads of figures that have been buried up to their necks in the earth. Generally this card means getting rid of the old to make way for the new.

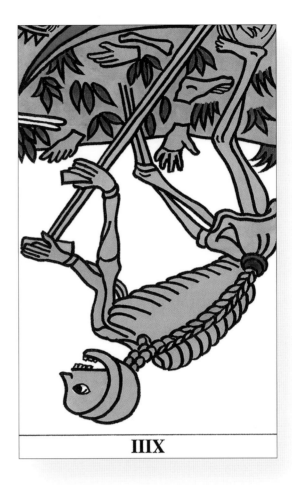

UPRIGHT

This signifies regeneration and rebirth, and the feeling that you have been given a brand new outlook on life and a fresh attitude on how to approach it. Sometimes this occurs when an unparalleled event takes place, such as a near-death experience.

REVERSED

This shows a refusal to let change happen, to let that which has run its course die. This can lead to a deep depression which may create the need to seek professional advice from a doctor, psychologist or experienced counsellor.

XIV Temperance

An angel-like figure holds two cups from which she pours liquid, one into the other. By the feet of the angel there is sometimes a pond of water. She has one foot placed in the pool and one foot placed on land. Temperance indicates moderation and blending of opposites.

UPRIGHT

You need to test the waters first, not dive in. Be patient and take things slowly. "Go carefully where angels fear to tread." Exert some self-control.

REVERSED

It is now time to stop and re-evaluate the situation before you proceed with anything further in order to stop making the same mistakes over again.

THE REALM OF CHANGING ISSUES

The seven cards of the final group of the Major Arcana are the most revered because they go beyond society and the individual. They represent universal laws that can alter the path of our lives.

XV The Devil

SIGN OF
CAPRICORN

A large figure, half-man and half-beast in appearance, stands on a pedestal. He has horns and the wings of a bat or bird. Two figures with horns, a man and a woman or sometimes lesser devils, are chained by heavy rope to the pedestal below him by the neck.

UPRIGHT

This indicates new-found passions, energy and enthusiasm. Rediscovering your innermost passions and having the energy and impetus to act on them.

REVERSED

Obsessions, addictions, and compulsive behaviour. When passion goes wrong or is directed in a negative manner, seeing a situation with any clarity is almost impossible.

XVII The Tower

A high tower is pictured being struck by a lightning bolt, which comes down from the sky. As a result of the explosion, the tower is destroyed, fire leaps from the tower and figures fall to their doom at the base of the building.

UPRIGHT

Complete and unforeseen disruptions and disagreements in life that are sudden or unplanned, and are therefore difficult to deal with. Abandoning past ties.

REVERSED

The worst of the disruptions are now over and it is time to piece your life back together in a way that is more suitable and positive.

XVII The Star

Many stars shine brightly in the night sky above a woman. In some decks a naked woman kneels down beside a pool of water. She holds two cups from which she pours liquid on to the land and back into the pool.

UPRIGHT

A wish come true, usually something you have thought of since childhood, such as meeting the perfect partner, or the ideal career opportunity.

REVERSED

What once seemed like a dream come true is no longer so appealing. Now that you have your desire, you wonder if it was worth it.

XVlll The Moon

Two dogs are barking up at a large shining moon in the sky. In front of them, a crayfish crawls from the water on to the land, and in the background are two towers, or pillars. In other decks a woman is pictured holding a crescent moon.

UPRIGHT

Take a close look behind the scenes as someone or something is not what it seems. There is a risk here that you are being lied to. Take another look at the situation and ask more questions.

REVERSED

When reversed, this card indicates that lies or deceptions are taking place. It would be best to become detached from a particular person or situation at this time because neither is likely to change.

XIX The Sun

A bright yellow sun shines down on two children or young people. Sometimes the children are pictured playing in a verdant garden of flowers. The Sun indicates the vitality of youth, happiness and a certain level of contentment.

UPRIGHT

An extremely positive card indicating growth and an increase of potential in all or many areas of life, such as progression in relationships, financial expansion, and physical growth (as in pregnancy).

REVERSED

Look at your life clearly, seeing it for what it actually is and not what you think it is. Re-evaluate your situation to make better progress and have a clearer sense of purpose and direction.

XX Judgement

An angel flies high above the earth blowing a trumpet. Below, three people rise from a tomb with their hands held together, pointed towards the sky. In the Visconti-Sforza deck, a godly figure appears at the top of the card. This card symbolizes an end of a situation and then rejuvenation and regeneration.

UPRIGHT

An indication that what has been holding you up and keeeping you in a rut is ending – a change will occur. You are now free to move forwards with a more positive demeanour and attitude. The lifting of karmic restrictions.

REVERSED

Poor judgement. This could keep you at a standstill or in a rut if you are not careful about the choices you make at this point. Take time to evaluate the direction you really want to take before proceeding.

XX1 The World

PLANET OF
SATURN

In some decks two children support a globe-like object. In other decks a hermaphroditic figure dances lightly as if on air. In both hands she holds white wands and around her there is a wreath with no join. From all four corners of the card the same four beasts that are present on the Wheel of Fortune card look inward towards the dancing figure.

UPRIGHT

This is by far the most auspicious card in the Tarot deck. It indicates great success for the individual in all areas of life. Total success and contentment are available to you now.

REVERSED

A fear of your own success in life. It is as though the goal is within reach, but you hesitate to take it – perhaps through fear of it not being quite deserved or fear of being disappointed.

The Minor Arcana

Although it is possible to do Tarot readings using only the Major Arcana cards, the story would not really be complete without the 56 cards of the Minor Arcana which correspond very closely with the cards in a modern deck of playing cards.

So far as we know, the Tarot was designed to be used as a total unit, comprising both the Major and Minor Arcana. The cards of the Major Arcana deal with life's grand gestures, showing us the main theme at a particular time. Its sister group, the Minor Arcana, completes the balance by showing us the finer and more ordinary details of our lives, such as the people, places, events and day-to-day circumstances.

THE FOUR SUITS

Each consisting of fourteen cards, the Minor Arcana is broken down into four separate suits, Swords, Wands, Pentacles and Cups, which correspond to Spades, Clubs, Diamonds and Hearts on a deck of playing cards. Their numerical order runs from ace to ten (pip cards), with four court cards, Page, Knight, Queen and King, to finish the sequence. Some modern Tarot decks use Prince and Princess cards as the Page and Knight.

The four suits deal with different, yet equally significant, areas and aspects of life. The suit of Cups deals with our emotions and issues that occur with love and relationships. The suit of Wands deals with physical actions and activities and our ambitions. The suit of Pentacles deals with all aspects of security, such as our finances, careers, home and family. And finally, the suit of Swords deals with moral issues and the conflicts that can arise as a result.

Although the cards of the Major Arcana have a dramatic impact, daily life is more likely to be made up of lots of little issues and incidents, some of which can seem quite insignificant. These are shown by the Minor Arcana. It is by combining these two distinct parts of the Tarot deck that you are given a more in-depth and realistic interpretation of life and its circumstances.

Above: The cards of the Minor Arcana are divided into four suits – Wands, Swords, Pentacles and Cups.

THE COURT CARDS

The four court cards of the Minor Arcana represent different people or personality traits. Although these cards stem from an old-fashioned and traditional view of male and female roles, the attributes discussed can be applied to anyone, regardless of age, gender, sexuality, race, or creed, unless specifically stated.

PAGES

In former times, pages were young people who worked in the royal courts, bringing messages, notices and letters. They served at the table, helped lords and ladies dress and did a multitude of other things. Being a page was the young person's education for a good position in life, hopefully leading to a knighthood. In the Tarot deck, the Pages are not specifically male or female. They can represent some or all of the following elements: children, messages, communication (such as telephone, letter, e-mail or another medium), information being given and passed on, studying or apprenticeship.

KNIGHTS

In the days of chivalry, the knights were young men who served the king and his court. They were sent out on errands, to find new lands, make new discoveries, forge new ties and test their skills. In the Tarot, the Knights are figures of action – whether the goal is self-discovery and finding your purpose in life, or challenging injustice on behalf of others. In today's society, where both men and women share the workplace and life's responsibilities, the Knights in the Tarot deck can represent either a male or female.

Above: Each suit in the Minor Arcana has four Court Cards. The meanings of these cards come from a traditional view of male and female roles, but can be applied to any gender.

QUEEN

The queen was the mature partner of the king. Queens will primarily represent women, and traditional female concerns: the home, relationships and emotional nurturing. A Queen in the Tarot deck can also represent a man who exhibits qualities or concerns in these areas.

KING

The king was the ruler of the land, whose duty was to maintain law and order. Kings will primarily represent men and traditional male concerns: ruling, responsibility and decision-making. A King in the Tarot deck can also represent a woman who exhibits qualities or concerns in these areas.

The Suit of Swords

When the Swords are present in a reading, the issues that are indicated by this suit concern any situations or actions to do with morality, moral conflict and conflicts in general. Think of an actual sword. It is sharply pointed, sometimes double-edged and made of strong metal, such as steel.

In the Arthurian legend, the young King Arthur was set a test: to pull the immovable sword, Excalibur, from a stone. Arthur, because of his fine character and upstanding moral convictions, is able to pull the sword free and with great ease. In doing so, he exhibited some of the qualities of the suit of Swords: notably, strength of character, determination and the ability to see an action through with an outstanding result.

The suit of Swords is related to the astrological element of Air. The three Air signs of the zodiac, Libra, Gemini and Aquarius,

Above: The Court Cards of Swords represent people who are strong, both physically and mentally.

are reflected in the suit of Swords. Like their astrological counterparts, this gives the people portrayed on the cards of Swords an analytical intellect. The thought behind the action is the key importance of this suit. In some foreign-language Tarot packs, the suit of Swords is called Epée, Schwerter or Espados. Swords equate to the suit of Spades in a pack of playing cards.

THE COURT CARDS OF SWORDS

Like a sharp sword made of steel, these characters tend to have a strong physical build with well-defined bone structure. Equally strong are their moral convictions and sense of right and wrong: these types will tend to look at life as black or white. They have a tendency to be serious and take their responsibilities in hand with great zeal and commitment.

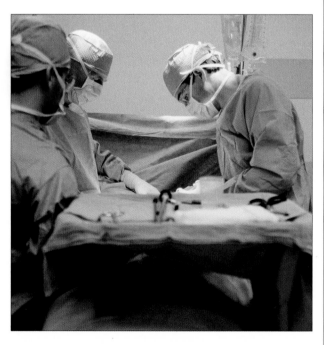

Above: The King of Swords represents someone who may have a demanding and responsible job, such as a surgeon.

Ace of Swords

UPRIGHT

Victory and triumph after difficulties. You have made a great achievement and you alone have done all the work. When the victory or triumph comes, it cannot be taken away because of all the hard work and struggle you have had to put in. Well-deserved success.

REVERSED

You must not put any more pressure on a person or situation, as you are in danger of pushing things over the edge. It would be best to sit back and allow the person or situation to calm down for a while even though it may be frustrating for you.

Two of Swords

UPRIGHT

Imposed self-protection. A wall is being put up between you and the outside world. This is usually due to upsetting situations which have taken place in the past, causing you to build up your defences to guard against the pain of the past, present or future.

REVERSED

You are being far too overprotective and not allowing anyone to get close to you. This is almost to the point of becoming a hermit. Try to be more open-minded.

43

Three of Swords

UPRIGHT

You may experience heartache through a love triangle: for example you, your husband and your lover; you, your mother and your sister; or you, your best friend and your girlfriend. Someone, if not all three people, will get hurt through choices that need to be made.

REVERSED

Indicates heartache through a love triangle as for the upright position but on a less serious scale. This may be due to disagreements, slight jealousies and insecurities, which can be resolved more easily.

Four of Swords

UPRIGHT

You need to take some time out to rest, recover and recuperate. This is in order to gather your energies for a difficult situation that lies ahead. This can also come up after a difficult situation, telling you there is a real need to rest now.

REVERSED

Now you have rested you are ready to take life and its challenges on again. You are able to enter the rat-race once more.

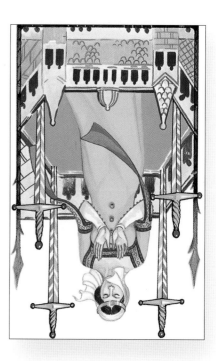

Five of Swords

UPRIGHT

A rift or argument has happened and you must deal with this. You have succeeded in proving an important point and your opinion has been heard and noted.

REVERSED

Now you have made your point, there is no need to be petulant and rub salt into the wounds or you could be accused of being ruthless.

Six of Swords

UPRIGHT

You are moving out of rough or anxious times and into smoother waters. Your situation or emotions will change. Life is on the up and problems will be dealt with more easily.

REVERSED

This card could indicate a delay or that your situation is improving, but not quite so smoothly or as quickly as you would like it to.

Seven of Swords

UPRIGHT
Through your pride or not knowing how to say "no", you are taking on more than you can handle and biting off more than you can chew. You need to be more diplomatic.

REVERSED
Certain pressures or problems that you have experienced in your life are now beginning to ease up.

Eight of Swords

UPRIGHT
There are restrictions on your ability to get on with your life freely. This could include, for example, living with a partner who is possessive, growing up with parents who have a severely strict outlook on life, or being restricted through disability, pregnancy, culture or faith.

REVERSED
The feelings of frustration or the restrictions that have been imposed on you are now being lifted, enabling you to move your life forwards and become more positive.

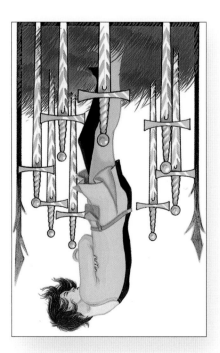

Nine of Swords

UPRIGHT

You are suffering from intense worries or stresses which may lead to sleepless nights. You feel overwhelmed by these anxieties.

REVERSED

The stresses or worries have intensified, leading to anxiety and fear. This is quite a serious problem at this stage and it is best to seek a professional opinion on such matters.

Ten of Swords

UPRIGHT

Your feelings have been deeply hurt from a situation or by a person that you were not expecting to be hurt by. This will be a painful experience but it will come to an end.

REVERSED

Great pain or heartache will be inflicted on you intentionally by a person or situation.

Page of Swords

UPRIGHT

A wonderful feeling of enthusiasm, excitement and a desire to take life head-on will come over you. This is similar to the kind of feeling you may have on New Year's Day.

REVERSED

A person is behaving frantically and impulsively, usually from great excitement.

Knight of Swords

UPRIGHT

An individual with great determination to achieve their goals, but also a person of great loyalty and conviction and strength of character. He or she will diligently pursue their aims whilst respecting and caring for others.

REVERSED

An individual whose zealous conviction has led them to behave erratically and brashly, at times stepping on other people's feelings with their cold and indifferent behaviour. Take care not to act irrationally.

Queen of Swords

UPRIGHT

This person is often a leader, keeping friends and family together, can be stubborn. Has few close friends, but those who have their loyalty, have it for life. They like clean-cut designs and styles of fashion. Strong, solid and reliable yet possibly aloof.

REVERSED

Similar to the upright Queen, but when reversed, can be extreme in their personality, harshly judging others. Can be unflinching in stubbornness and could be accused of "cutting off their nose to spite their face". Difficult to get close to, and may appear cold.

King of Swords

UPRIGHT

A person who prefers the known, often with a fixed routine. Extremely loyal, has a strong sense of responsibility – will not let people down. Sensible yet emotional, does not wear their heart on their sleeve. Conservative in looks, likes clean cuts, and practical designs.

REVERSED

Can be too regimented in their routines. Harsh judge of anything that does not fit into clear stereotypes. Perhaps has a narrow outlook. Similar in appearance to the upright King. Intolerance and narrow-mindedness are key here – you may meet someone like this.

The Suit of Wands

When Wands are present in a reading, the issues that can occur under this suit are connected with physical activity and action. Wands are concerned with the "here and now" – situations and plans that are being actioned in the present time. You can think of Wands as the "Go, go, go!" suit, because whenever these cards show up in a reading there is usually a lot of hubbub and activity surrounding them. Wands indicate a creative energy and sometimes an extrovert quality. They are also associated with intuition. The suit of Wands is related to the element of Fire, and it is this element that puts the action and imagination into the Wands. Aries, Leo and Sagittarius are the three fire signs of the zodiac that are connected to this suit.

Other names for this suit are Rods, Staves, Sceptres, Sticks or Batons. In some foreign-language Tarot packs, Wands are called Bastoni, Stabe or Bastos. They equate to the playing card suit of Clubs.

Above: The suit of Wands is connected to action, energy and movement in a physical or creative sense.

THE COURT CARDS OF WANDS

Wands are batons made from wood. Wands are associated with people who are at ease with communication: they have quick and clear speech and are often interested in higher learning or cultural interests. They are also "people's people". As the suit of Wands is the Fire suit and fire is active and always on the move, so the Wands are also physically active and may have a wiry or athletic physique. They can be exotic to look at, with interesting, attractive faces. They tend to have a healthy complexion with a nice flush of colour. Their hair may have reddish or golden tones to it, with a natural curl or wave.

Left: The Knight of Wands represents a healthy, active person who is always keen to try new activities.

Ace of Wands

UPRIGHT

Put quite simply, the time to act on an idea is now. If you are planning any ventures or special tasks, now is the time to get things moving. Karmically speaking, this moment in time is most auspicious for the future of any given project or issue.

REVERSED

Plans or projects are currently put on hold or there is a lack of interest. Although it may be frustrating to wait, it is not the right time to proceed at the moment and it is more advantageous to wait until the timing intuitively feels better.

Two of Wands

UPRIGHT

Now is a good time to bring new people into your life and to share what you have to offer. Expanding our circle of friends and contacts can increase our happiness, because life can be quite meaningless without someone else or others to share it with.

REVERSED

Someone who is living a solitary life and not finding happiness in that life. Now is the time to become more socially involved, perhaps by taking up activities that involve a varied group of people. The alternative is to face the reality of living life alone.

Three of Wands

UPRIGHT

It is time to pursue new interests or directions. A new path is opening up and if you go down it, it will bring positive things into your life. This could indicate taking up higher learning, a hobby, or beginning to research a subject that interests you.

REVERSED

You are too passive, waiting for life to happen and any new directions to become absolutely obvious. It is time to formulate new directions and ideas about the path that you can follow. Decide what it is you are interested in, or good at, and take action.

Four of Wands

UPRIGHT

There is a warm and festive feeling in your life at the moment. Now is a good time to emphasize your feeling of goodwill by getting friends and family together to share in these positive vibrations. This could be through a weekend away or a party.

REVERSED

You feel fed up with the general feeling of inertia and boredom in your life. You need to move yourself out of the rut by taking physical action, such as changing your scenery by taking a holiday, redecorating, or doing something completely new.

Five of Wands

UPRIGHT

Discussions and mild debates are taking place at the moment in order to clear the air on certain subjects or issues. Usually these discussions are beneficial and can lead to greater harmony and understanding between the parties involved.

REVERSED

This card indicates that there is a degree of discord and disharmony in current discussions or negotiations. Consequently, the matter that is under discussion will require time and patience before it is resolved.

Six of Wands

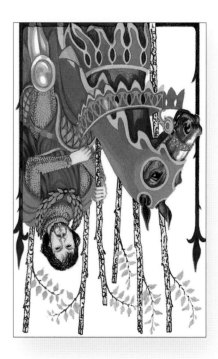

UPRIGHT

You will receive public recognition and admiration for a job that is well done. Your peer group and those closest to you give you good support for your actions. You feel satisfied with your efforts.

REVERSED

This card indicates that you will finally receive the recognition due to you for a good deed or achievement in the past. You will be given thanks for your previous efforts and a task well done.

Seven of Wands

UPRIGHT

You will need to protect and defend your current position in life. It's time to watch out for the competition in a personal or professional capacity, but provided you keep on guard and have your wits about you, you should have no problems.

REVERSED

This card shows that your defences are down and you have feelings of self-doubt. You are in danger of being caught off-guard by someone or something in either a personal or professional capacity.

Eight of Wands

UPRIGHT

Life is moving in the fast lane. Look and see which cards fall next to this card in a reading, as their course of action will be speeded up. For example, the Lovers next to the Eight would be a relationship happening quickly, or the World next to the Eight would mean success is imminent.

REVERSED

Things have slowed down in your life and are grinding to a halt or you may feel misdirected. Re-evaluate your current position in case you are unsure or confused before pushing ahead with new ideas and directions.

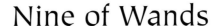

Nine of Wands

UPRIGHT

There is a chance that you are being overly defensive or suspicious and in danger of becoming paranoid about a current person, event or situation. It is best to examine your feelings quite carefully before you over-react dramatically.

REVERSED

Your suspicions have been verified and it is time to move on in your life. The best advice is to look to the future and not to get too engrossed or involved in the problems of the past.

Ten of Wands

UPRIGHT

You are currently going through a lot of stresses and strains. You have many responsibilities but you are quite capable of handling them so don't worry too much.

REVERSED

The stresses and strains of recent times have now subsided and you are beginning to feeling more contented. You can now relax and start to take things easy.

Page of Wands

UPRIGHT

The Page indicates news coming to you, by post, telephone, or e-mail for example. It is information that will be of special interest and significance to you.

REVERSED

Precisely the same as the definition for an upright position, except that the news or information you receive will be coming from someone who is younger than yourself.

Knight of Wands

UPRIGHT

A person who is soul-searching, looking for answers as to why they are here on earth. Until they find what they are looking for, it is futile to try and pin them down in a relationship. Wait and you will be rewarded with a life-long friend or partner.

REVERSED

A person chaotically looking for answers to their existence. They never settle in one place or with one person long enough to understand anything about life's meaning. Such chaos can lead to outbursts of temper. Can be too extreme in their passions.

Queen of Wands

UPRIGHT

A person who craves being centre of attention. Uses their charms to better themselves. Often exotic in looks, prefers striking colours or fashions. Crafty with their hands as well as their mind. Would do well to go into a career such as sales, or the theatre.

REVERSED

Similar to the upright Queen, but when reversed, becomes competitive and manipulative in order to be centre of attention. May put value on what they can gain and not on people. Not good at keeping secrets – they may reveal them to score popularity points.

King of Wands

UPRIGHT

A person who is non-judgemental and deals with issues easily. Has a giving nature. Needs to be in touch with nature to feel grounded. A good partner or friend to those who appreciate their relaxed philosophy. Typical features include wavy hair with golden tints and a healthy build.

REVERSED

Similar to the upright King, but when reversed, rather eccentric. Perhaps an inventor who isolates himself while he creates. Has no "people skills" and does not understand humanity. Can appear intolerant or narrow-minded.

The Suit of Pentacles

When the Pentacles are present in a reading, the issues that fall under this suit are to do with security and the material elements of life. This is echoed by the shape of the pentacle itself which is a gold disk that symbolizes money.

The aspects of life covered by Pentacles concern such things as career, investments, family, marriage, children, home, and any of those things in life which give us stability or a sense of belonging.

The suit of Pentacles is related to the element of Earth and the issues that come up with this suit relate to our senses and things that ground us. The three Earth signs of the zodiac connected with this suit are

Above: The suit of Pentacles (or coins) relates to the financial and material aspects of our lives.

Taurus, Virgo and Capricorn. The Pentacles can also be referred to as Disks, Coins, Money or Circles. In some foreign-language packs, they are called Deniers, Denari, Munzen or Oros. They equate to the playing card suit of Diamonds.

THE COURT CARDS OF PENTACLES

The symbol of the golden pentacle or coin signifies money and security, and the material side of life. The people represented by Pentacles are generally concerned, therefore, with matters of security. They tend to be very family-oriented and are focused on all the trappings of a secure life, such as a good job with a strong career path, a stable home environment, having more than enough food in the cupboards, money in the bank and so on. In appearance they tend to have a solid build, eyes that are deep-set and, more often then not, their hair colour is any shade of brown.

Above: The Page of Pentacles can indicate that you may receive a gift, an inheritance or winnings of some kind.

Ace of Pentacles

UPRIGHT

Great financial rewards or success concerning a security issue. This could be a windfall or inheritance, or the feeling of finally achieving success in your career. This is also the perfect card to indicate total success in a relationship, security and contentment.

REVERSED

A reversal of fortune that involves your financial situation or perhaps a relationship. This is a time of feeling "at your lowest point" and of experiencing the inner emptiness that can arise when there is no real security in your life.

Two of Pentacles

UPRIGHT

You need to keep your balancing act up for a bit longer. Don't make any decision to drop any one aspect of your life just yet: you will need more information before making that choice.

REVERSED

You are in a situation that is difficult to balance and you are in danger of losing control. Assessing then organizing your priorities would help considerably at this time.

Three of Pentacles

UPRIGHT

Signatures on contracts or important paperwork. This could be a marriage certificate, an employment contract, mortgage or loan documents, or divorce papers, for example.

REVERSED

There will be a delay in signing contracts or official documents at this time. You could feel very frustrated.

Four of Pentacles

UPRIGHT

You have real fears about finances and feel a need to hold on to your money. Perhaps you have had times in your life where you have experienced financial stresses. This has left you with an underlying insecurity towards financial matters in general.

REVERSED

You may feel deeply insecure in financial matters. This may stem from a cause in the past that has left you fearful of spending money even when financially secure. Pay attention to emotional matters and don't lose sight of the important aspects.

Five of Pentacles

UPRIGHT

This card warns of a financial disaster or loss of security of some kind that has occurred recently or else is on the way, such as a job loss, bankruptcy, divorce, losing your home, or general money losses of some kind.

REVERSED

The financial or security loss has already taken place and you may feel a sense of helplessness. The task of putting things back together should be taken in hand and progressed.

Six of Pentacles

UPRIGHT

You will be looked after or treated fairly regarding a security issue. An indication of generosity in a financial transaction, settlement or award, such as a large pay rise, a profitable house sale, a generous divorce or court settlement, for example.

REVERSED

You may receive unfair treatment around a security issue – not receiving a well-deserved pay rise, an unfair divorce or court settlement, or a poor return on a house sale. You are not happy about the outcome.

Seven of the Pentacles

UPRIGHT

Now is a good time to spoil yourself or make an investment and get the benefits of your hard work. You may have some anxieties about money but this would not have any adverse effect on your finances at this time.

REVERSED

It is time to stop "saving up for a rainy day". This attitude towards your finances is no longer appropriate: now it is time to do something special for yourself.

Eight of Pentacles

UPRIGHT

You have a talent with your hands that could earn you financial rewards and, if developed to a high level of skill, could even become a career. This card refers to any person who works with their hands, such as an artist, photographer, healer or writer.

REVERSED

The talent is there in your hands, but it still needs some fine tuning. You may need to go on to higher learning or to practise your skill more often, so that you become proficient enough to proceed with a proper career in the given field of interest.

Nine of Pentacles

UPRIGHT

A person who has a natural demeanour to attract a good lifestyle to themselves. They look competent and well cared for. If they have a partner, they are most likely to be successful.

REVERSED

This card indicates a person who at times can be ruthless in obtaining a good lifestyle. They may marry or have an affair with someone purely for money.

Ten of Pentacles

UPRIGHT

An established secure home, family or relationship. This can also indicate the actual building of a home, which is usually an older property in pleasant surroundings, where several generations of the family will enjoy its homely atmosphere.

REVERSED

This card indicates disharmony or an interference in a usually secure, established home, such as petty quarrels, family feuds and potential disorganization. There could also be instability regarding the family and finances.

Page of Pentacles

UPRIGHT

News or information about security is coming your way. This may be a win of money, a birthday gift or a small inheritance. It may be that you hear of a job vacancy, and you get the job, or you have news about a pay rise.

REVERSED

This card indicates that a person younger than yourself is giving you news or information in relation to security.

Knight of Pentacles

UPRIGHT

This person is determined to get ahead with their ambitions in life. They plan strategically, knowing exactly how to climb the ladder of success and will proceed to take the necessary steps to achieve their goal. This is a focussed person.

REVERSED

Similar to the upright Knight, but with the added element of ruthlessness. Moreover, these types will tend to burn their bridges as they continue to move up in the world, thereby making plenty of enemies along the way.

Queen of Pentacles

UPRIGHT

A person with strong maternal and material instincts. Whether or not they have children, they make people welcome in their home. Domestic life is important – they often choose marriage and children. They work hard to make their surroundings comfortable.

REVERSED

This person goes ruthlessly towards their goals, letting nothing or no one stand in their way. Often a reflection of a very insecure or unstable childhood. They over-compensate for security and love by chasing and obtaining financial success.

King of Pentacles

UPRIGHT

A successful, powerful person with a sense of responsibility. Has often had someone else to provide for. Not overconfident. Measures achievements through the security of family and views themself through relationships. Will usually make a caring partner.

REVERSED

Similar to the upright card, but reversed this King has a huge chip on their shoulder. Insecure about their role as a protector, perhaps due to a failure. Finds it hard to let go of the past. This can make forming new relationships difficult. Can indicate weakness.

The Suit of Cups

When the suit of Cups is present in a reading, the issues are connected with love, our emotions and intuitive faculties. The symbol of the cup resembles a chalice or sacred drinking vessel and brings to mind the Holy Grail, or the "cup of life" itself. Consequently the issues of the Cups cards have a spiritual quality to them, affecting our emotional and intuitive selves: they are about self-acceptance and self-love as well as love for another.

The suit of Cups is represented by the element of Water and, like water, our emotions are influenced by the Moon. The Moon is powerful and mysterious, able to influence the tides of the planet. Just as the Moon waxes and wanes, so our moods constantly shift and change and our emotional lives are in a constant state of flux like the waters of the ocean. The three Water signs of the zodiac that are reflected in the suit of Cups are Cancer, Scorpio and Pisces.

Other names for the suit of Cups are Chalices or Goblets. In some Tarot packs they may be called Coupes, Coppe, Kelche or Copas. They equate to the playing card suit of Hearts.

Above: The Suit of Cups is connected to issues involving our emotional well-being, such as our relationships with others.

Above: The Court Cards of Cups represent gentle people who are often nurturing, loving and caring.

THE COURT CARDS OF CUPS

The legendary cup of the Holy Grail is alleged to contain the waters of eternal life – one sip is enough to replenish, nourish and fulfil us all as humans. The people of Cups can be nourishing in a similar way, with kind and loving natures. They are deeply emotional people and usually spiritual. They need love in their lives to feel alive and may put love before life itself. Their gentle natures do not know the meaning of the word "no" and they find it hard to hurt the people they care about.

Physically these types are sensual and usually attractive to look at. With soft skin and no sharp-angled bones protruding, they give the appearance of softness and fleshiness. Often their hair is fine and billowy, and they have large gentle eyes with great empathy. They prefer to wear delicate and sensual colours, such as purples, blues, silvers, creams and shades of burgundies and pinks. They will choose their clothes by texture, liking such fabrics as plush velvets, silks and linens, for example. They prefer jewellery that is unique in its setting, and have a liking for antique or specially designed pieces.

Ace of Cups

UPRIGHT

Known as The Holy Grail or "cup of life". Some readers consider it to be the most important card in the deck. Indicates a miracle or a blessing, like finding a soulmate, or conceiving a baby. Any situation that this card is near will be blessed with good fortune.

REVERSED

Denotes disappointment, sadness, or a person with a "God Complex", believing the world revolves around them. With a huge ego this person tends to fall quite hard. They need to come back down to earth and accept other people's views and feelings.

Two of Cups

UPRIGHT

The forming of an important relationship. The relationship is one built on common interests, friendship and a higher understanding of adult love and companionship. Usually it will span the march of time and grow and develop with you.

REVERSED

An argument or disagreement has taken place between two parties that is really quite petty. One or the other party in the relationship needs to break the ice and make the important first move towards reconciliation.

Three of Cups

UPRIGHT

This card denotes rejoicing, optimism and growth. It is a good time to enjoy yourself and indicates formal celebrations of events such as weddings, anniversaries, christenings, or a promotion.

REVERSED

Formal celebrations will meet with some discord. This may arise through personality conflicts or bad timing in communications, such as things being said that would have been better dealt with at a different time and place.

Four of Cups

UPRIGHT

An offer of an emotional nature will be put to you, but it will come with strings attached. It would be wise to first find out what these strings are before accepting the offer.

REVERSED

You may be the victim of feeling that "the grass is greener on the other side" and have now got yourself emotionally involved in a situation that is not as good as it first seemed.

Five of Cups

UPRIGHT

A situation needs emotional sacrifice, such as deciding between husband and children or a lover. In this case the lover is sacrificed due to family commitment. Or a new friend is causing problems with you and an old friend – the new friend is sacrificed.

REVERSED

A similar type of sacrifice needs to be made, but it is less heart-rending. For example, choosing between a hobby or your full-time career. Your career needs more of your time and commitment, so it might be the hobby that will have to be sacrificed.

Six of Cups

UPRIGHT

This card shows that you are currently dealing with memories, such as those connected with a person from the past, childhood issues or even with children themselves.

REVERSED

Similar to the upright meaning except that in this case it indicates the recent past. You will be dealing with someone or a memory from the recent past, roughly within the last five years.

Seven of Cups

UPRIGHT

This card indicates that there are plenty of appealing opportunities on offer to you currently. Indeed, there are so many of them that you may be unsure of which one to choose. Whichever one you take up, however, will prove very rewarding and emotionally fulfilling.

REVERSED

Emotionally you are feeling in a bit of a rut and there seems to be nothing that fascinates you at the moment. Do not worry, this barren emotional time will pass and there will be new experiences just around the corner.

Eight of Cups

UPRIGHT

All that has been familiar to you emotionally has gone past its "sell-by date". For example, you realize that the relationship you have been in for five years is not for you anymore. You decide to leave it, and its comforts. This is about venturing into the world alone, but being relieved to do so.

REVERSED

You are on the path of finding yourself and are able to re-evaluate the past more clearly, enabling you to abandon old habits or friendships that are not working and to move forwards to the future more positively.

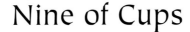

Nine of Cups

UPRIGHT

You are feeling a sense of emotional abundance, sensuality and fulfilment, that "all is right with the world". This feeling is quite similar to the emotional bliss that some women experience when they are pregnant.

REVERSED

This card denotes complacency. Emotionally you are quite spoilt and maybe taking for granted the love you receive from others. There may also be the feeling that you are never satisfied with your life.

Ten of Cups

UPRIGHT

A fresh, new start in the home. This can be an actual new home, or introducing a new aspect to the existing one – such as a child, a new partner, or even making structural changes to the property, which will make it feel completely different, fresh and new.

REVERSED

You will experience stress on the domestic front due to a disruption or a new introduction into the home. These stresses, although hard work, will usually work themselves through given some time and patience.

Page of Cups

UPRIGHT

This card is always present in a reading when a person is trying to gain your affection or attention. It is common for it to come up when you are dating a new person, or when it is your birthday, or when someone close is trying to make up after a disagreement. This card is informally known as "The Courtship Card".

REVERSED

The reversed card is very similar to the upright definition of the Page of Cups, except that the attention will come from a person younger than yourself.

Knight of Cups

UPRIGHT

You are being wooed. This card can indicate a lover. It concerns matters of the heart, whether this is an actual love affair or other things such as artistic self-expression. Perhaps a new partner is putting on their best behaviour to court you.

REVERSED

A person will be flirtatious, wanting affection due to lack of self-worth. More often than not love is a sport for them, in which they are adept at convincing you that they're worth falling in love with. This person tends to be lax with the truth.

Queen of Cups

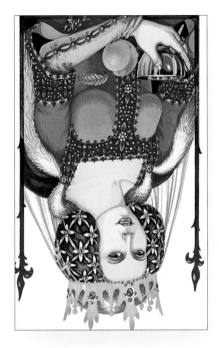

UPRIGHT

This person has an ability to listen to others, is interested in what they say. Captivating and naturally charming, they have a sensual, understated look that attracts others. The Queen of Cups makes a wonderful partner, friend, parent and colleague.

REVERSED

Similar to the upright Queen, except now plagued by deeply-rooted insecurity, doubting themself and their appearance. They may stay in relationships and friendships where their good nature is taken advantage of and they are taken for granted.

Kings of Cups

UPRIGHT

This person enjoys socializing and people in general. They are at their best when they have an audience that appreciates them. Creative and drawn to the world of art, theatre and music. They have great presence, a vibrant personality, and wear bright colours and showy styles.

REVERSED

Like the reversed Queen, this person suffers from deep insecurities and has a tendency to form destructive relationships. They will go to great lengths to get attention. They need to watch out for depression.

A quick guide to the Minor Arcana

This numerical guide can be used as a reference to the Minor Arcana definitions. Use the charts to take the general background definition of a particular suit and cross-reference it with the generic numerical meaning for any card. As an example, take the Nine of Cups. The definition for the suit of Cups concerns emotional and intuitive issues, whilst a general definition for any number nine card in the Tarot deck concerns poise and contentment. By combining this information, you can work out a general definition, which signifies emotional contentment in your or the querent's (the individual receiving the reading) current life.

	ACE	TWO	THREE	FOUR	FIVE	SIX
Swords Epees, Spade, Espados. Playing card suit: Spades. Element: Air. Suit of Swords deals with future or present moral conflicts or battles.	Upright: A hard battle will be won Reversed: Pushing too hard now will not be effective	Upright: Self-protection Reversed: Over self-protection	Upright: Heartache Reversed: Heartache but less severe	Upright: Recovery and rest Reversed: Reactivating life	Upright: Proving a point Reversed: Petulant behaviour	Upright: Situation improving Reversed: Delay in situation improving
Wands Batons, Rods, Staves. Playing card suit: Clubs. Element: Fire. Suit of Wands deals with progression, plans being actioned, present time.	Upright: Your potential for success is now Reversed: Wait to action plans	Upright: New people will be coming into life Reversed: A lonely individual	Upright: New direction Reversed: Lonely individual	Upright: Warm, festive environment Reversed: Feeling of boredom	Upright: Discussion or debates Reversed: Discord in discussion or debates	Upright: Situation improving Reversed: Finally being recognized for past good deed
Pentacles Coins, Dealer, Disks. Playing card suit: Diamonds. Element: Earth. Suit of Pentacles deals with home, security, family, career, money.	Upright: Great security in work, home or family Reversed: Feeling insecure in work, home or family	Upright: Balancing issues Reversed: Losing control over issues	Upright: Signatures or contracts Reversed: Signatures or contracts being delayed	Upright: Fear of financial ruin or poverty Reversed: Paranoia of financial ruin or poverty	Upright: Financial or security loss Reversed: Loss has already occurred	Upright: Being treated fairly Reversed: Unfair treatment
Cups Coupes, Chalices, Grails. Playing card suit: Hearts. Element: Water. Suit of Cups deals with emotions, emotional issues and love.	Upright: A blessing or miracle Reversed: Someone who believes themselves to be godlike	Upright: Important relationship or companionship Reversed: Disagreements in important relationship	Upright: Formal celebrations Reversed: Discord in formal celebrations	Upright: Offer with strings attached Reversed: Situation feeling uncomfortable	Upright: Emotional sacrifices Reversed: Less heart-rending sacrifice	Upright: Past memories, childhood or children Reversed: More recent memories

SEVEN	EIGHT	NINE	TEN	PAGE	KNIGHT	QUEEN	KING
Upright: Taking on too much Reversed: Pressure easing	Upright: Restrictions Reversed: Restrictions lifted	Upright: Worry and stress Reversed: Anxiety and fear	Upright: Hurt and pain Reversed: Extreme hurt and pain	Upright: Feeling of enthusiasm Reversed: Impulsiveness	Upright: A determined individual Reversed: An over-zealous individual	Upright: Strongly moralled, a female leader Reversed: A harsh judgemental woman	Upright: A strongly moralled male leader Reversed: A harsh judgemental man
Upright: Defend current position Reversed: Being caught off guard	Upright: Actions being sped up Reversed: Actions being slowed down	Upright: Being overly suspicious Reversed: Suspicions confirmed	Upright: Stress and strains Reversed: Stress and strains easing	Upright: News being received Reversed: News being received by a younger person	Upright: A person soul-searching Reversed: A person chaotically soul-searching	Upright: A captivating and dramatic woman Reversed: A competitive, manipulative woman	Upright: Nature loving man Reversed: An eccentric man
Upright: Good time to spend or invest Reversed: Treat yourself to something special	Upright: A talent which can lead to financial rewards Reversed: A talent that needs fine tuning	Upright: A person who attracts a good life style Reversed: A person who loves purely for financial gain	Upright: An established secure home Reversed: Disharmony in an established secure home	Upright: News of security or money coming forward Reversed: News of security or money coming from a younger person	Upright: An ambitious person, wanting to progress Reversed: A ruthlessly ambitious person wanting to progress	Upright: A woman with strong maternal instincts Reversed: A ruthless career woman	Upright: Responsible, successful man Reversed: A man who cannot let go of the past
Upright: Opportunities Reversed: Opportunities lie ahead	Upright: Emotionally walking away Reversed: Have already emotionally walked away	Upright: Emotionally fulfilled Reversed: Emotionally unfulfilled	Upright: New aspect to home or new home Reversed: Discord in home	Upright: Card of courtship Reversed: A younger person giving attention	Upright: Romantic attention being given Reversed: A flirtatious person seeking attention	Upright: A caring, emotional, feminine woman Reversed: An insecure and over-emotional woman	Upright: A social and sensual man Reversed: An insecure, attention-grabbing man

Reading the Tarot for meditation and self-guidance

The Tarot can make an excellent self-help tool and can be put to use for purposes such as meditation, self-analysis and looking into one's own issues.

THE TAROT AND MEDITATION

This exercise is intended for use in focusing thought patterns and clearing the mind of the external and sometimes negative aspects of the world. It also helps the mind to focus internally on a particular area of life, a thought or a feeling that your intuition may be telling you needs to be looked at specifically.

Firstly choose an environment which is calm, restful and disruption-free. You could have tranquil music playing in the background if you find this relaxes you and helps you to concentrate. Sit comfortably at a table or on a cushion on the floor with the Tarot deck in hand and gently shuffle the deck. Once you feel that the the deck is nicely shuffled, fan the cards out in front of you, face downwards, then from the fan of cards pick one out and turn it face upward. Read the card's title and take in the visual imagery.

Once you have studied the card and all its details sufficiently, place the card back down in front of you, face downwards, and close your eyes. Relax and let the imagery you have just been studying freely enter your mind's eye, and let it take you into whatever visual world the mind creates. Continue the process of meditation for as long as you want to.

Above: The Tarot deck can be used as a tool for self-guidance. Study the cards in a quiet and calm environment.

Knowing the right time to finish a meditation is a personal matter and can only be decided by the individual undertaking it.

TAROT FOR SELF-ANALYSIS

Firstly choose an environment that is calm and interruption-free. Then decide on the question to be asked of oneself, such as "Do I overreact to problems?" or perhaps "Am I too clingy in my relationships?" or any series of introspective questions that could be applied. Keeping the question in the back of your mind, shuffle the deck of Tarot cards, stopping when you feel comfortable that it is time to do so. From the top of the deck draw three cards and lay them down in a horizontal row in front of you, picture side up. Interpret the three definitions on the cards in order to formulate an answer to or discussion about the question. Put special emphasis on the central or middle card of the row, as this will be the defining answer to the question.

For example, laid out in front of you could be The Fool, the Six of Cups and the Page of Swords and the question asked could be "Do I overreact to problems?" The Six of Cups may indicate it has been a problem suffered from since childhood and/or that one reacts in a childish or overdramatic way towards problems. The Fool may signify a hasty or changeable nature and the Page of Swords could signify that although an overreaction to problems does take place, a positive and upbeat reaction also occurs.

LOOKING INTO AN ISSUE

Follow the same procedure as you would for Tarot for self-analysis. Decide on the area of life or issue in question, such as "Will my new job be a rewarding experience?" or "Is my relationship going to get through this difficult period?" or perhaps "Would moving house be a good idea at the moment?"

With a question in mind, shuffle the deck whilst concentrating on the issue or subject. Stop when you feel that it's comfortable and right to do so. Place the Tarot deck down in front of you, draw three cards out from the top and lay them down in a horizontal row in order to interpret and formulate a response to your question. With this type of analysis, read and interpret all three cards together. This will help in looking into the aspects or angles of an issue or subject that may not have been considered previously. In this case, the three cards signify aspects of an issue or subject; they do not directly signify an answer.

If, for example, the question asked was "Will my new job be a rewarding experience?" and the cards laid out in front of you were the Eight of Wands, the Four of Wands and The Sun, these cards could signify a warm informal environment (Four of Wands) in which rapid (Eight of Wands) growth (The Sun) takes place.

The thing to remember with any self-analysis or development exercise is to enjoy the process and keep in mind that the decisions taken in life can only be made for you by yourself.

Above: As well as general guidance, the Tarot cards can provide help with specific questions or problems.

Reading the Tarot for others

Almost as much energy needs to be put into choosing the setting for a reading as it does in interpreting the definitions within the reading itself. Firstly it is vital to set the right ambience. This must be a calm and uninterrupted space, be it indoors or outside. It should be an environment free from the distractions of other people and noises, and must be free of any chaos in general. Choose a comfortable place to sit, both for the reader and the querent, with a table or a flat space to lay the cards upon, and, if required, relaxing melodic music in the background.

A relaxed setting for this undertaking is vital due to the intimate and private subject areas that may be discussed between reader and querent in a typical Tarot reading. Eye contact and a caring approach will allow the querent to feel at ease while they are having their cards read.

The querent should concentrate on the subject or issue of their reading. At the same time, they should handle the cards, shuffling them in some way. Remember to advise the querent on the best way to do this, as some Tarot decks are large and they may have difficulty handling them if their hands are small.

As soon as the querent feels they have concentrated on and handled the cards for long enough, they can stop. This process will be different for each individual. Some people

Above: It is important that you put the querent at ease so that they feel relaxed and happy before the reading begins.

will take only a short time to get their issues clear in their mind, whilst others will take longer to focus. It must be left up to the querent to decide when they are ready. They should then pass you the deck.

Sometimes during the shuffling process some cards may become reversed. This is caused by the querent either subconsciously or deliberately turning the Tarot cards around or accidentally dropping a few and putting them back in reversed amongst the Tarot deck.

Left: Once the querent feels happy that they have shuffled the cards enough, they should pass the deck back to the reader.

Either way, it is the individual's unique handling of the cards that will determine how they fall when they are passed over to the reader to be laid out in a spread and interpreted. If the querent asks when they should hand the cards over, it is best to tell them to do so when they feel they are ready. At this point, when the complete Tarot deck has been placed back into the hands of the reader, the process of laying out the cards or Tarot spread takes place and the interpretation of the definitions of the cards occurs. This is the reading.

Left: Tarot readings can take place anywhere you feel comfortable. A quiet outdoor setting can provide calm.

Let the querent know that it may take a few moments of silence to access the information laid out before you and that you will begin shortly to interpret the cards for them. This way you will avoid any uncomfortable silences. If it is the querent's first time having a Tarot reading, remember that the experience may feel somewhat awkward or peculiar for them.

If you are just beginning the study of the Tarot cards and how to read them, it is important to convey this fact to the querent. This will take away some of the pressure from the reader. The querent may feel comforted in the knowledge that the experience is new and unfamiliar to the reader too.

When you finish a reading, always ask the querent if they have understood and accept the information you have given them, and be prepared to expand on matters or answer any questions they might have. It is with this final step that you will be able to monitor your own skill as a reader and learn how to read the cards

more effectively. For instance, perhaps everything that you said was true – then great! This will give you a real boost of confidence. Or maybe some of what you said was incorrect – the querent will let you know either way.

Even if the whole reading was incorrect, do not worry and remember you are still learning and that everyone learns through their mistakes – even the most experienced Tarot reader can get it wrong sometimes. The key is in the caring communication of issues, and the discretion and consideration with which you handle the person who is sitting in front of you having the reading.

Above: Different lighting effects, such as candles, can be used to create the right atmosphere for a reading.

Step-by-step Tarot reading

1 Clear your mind – try to let go of all of your own personal problems or issues. This will get easier with time, although if you have difficulty doing this now, try focusing your mind on one pleasant thing, such as a rainbow or a sunrise.

2 Organize the cards – make sure all the cards are in the upright position before giving them to the querent. If he or she, through their handling of the deck, reverses certain cards that is their own choice. To give the querent someone else's reversed cards is unfair, as their reading would then be influenced by the choices of the previous person who handled the cards.

3 Shuffle the cards – it is vital to do this as it gives the cards a fresh start. The Tarot cards are larger than normal playing cards, so doing this this may take some practice. Make sure you focus on keeping your mind clear while doing this.

4 The querent picks the main issue – ask the querent to concentrate their mind as clearly as possible on the issues or areas of life that they are currently concerned about. These will be the areas you will be interpreting for them during the reading.

5 The querent shuffles the pack – hand the querent the Tarot deck and ask them to shuffle the cards. They should concentrate on the issues they want to look into. When they feel they have shuffled the cards enough, they should hand the deck back. It is important that they do this when they feel ready: remember you are interpreting for another person and their issues.

6 Lay out a spread – using whichever spread you are the most comfortable with, draw your cards from the top of the deck. Lay them down in the correct sequence, face up. As you become more experienced, you can learn more sequences and vary these.

7 Read the cards – remember you are starting to learn and understand the Tarot. Let the querent know that you are a beginner. If what you are interpreting does not make sense or the subject is delicate, it is best to use discretion and plead ignorance to take the pressure off.

8 Drawing to a conclusion – when you have ascertained and interpreted all you can from the Tarot cards, let the querent know that you have finished the reading. Ask them if they have understood and accepted the information you have given them.

The Celtic Cross spread

The Celtic Cross is the best Tarot spread to use when you have a specific question on your mind, such as "I have just had a job interview – will I get the job?" This spread is best used when you are looking for an answer to a question that can be clearly answered with a "yes" or "no". This is because it deals with one issue at a time. Lay the cards out following the order of the sequence shown. The position of each card refers to a different issue as listed below:

1 PERSON IN QUESTION
The card in this position indicates the querent.

2 POSSIBILITIES OR PROBLEMS
This will either indicate possibilities for a solution and a positive way forwards, or problems that may occur along the way.

3 BEST COURSE OF ACTION
This shows the best course of action or the road to follow in order to achieve the desired outcome.

4 INFLUENCES FROM THE PAST
This card is about a person or something from the querent's past that is present now or affecting the current situation.

5 CURRENT ATMOSPHERE
This represents the mood of the situation. This may be light and positive or heavy and serious.

6 SHORT-TERM FUTURE
This represents how the situation will develop over the next three months.

Right: Practise laying out the cards in the correct sequence.

7 PRESENT STATE OF THE SITUATION
This tells us whether or not the current situation is precarious or stable. It indicates where it is now in relation to the future outcome.

8 OUTSIDE INFLUENCES
This represents other people or issues that may have an effect on the desired outcome or that need to be taken into consideration.

9 HOME ENVIRONMENT
This tells us something about the querent's home environment at the present time.

10 THE QUERENT'S SUBCONSCIOUS FEELINGS
This indicates whether the querent feels positive or negative about the situation and its possible outcome.

11 LONG-TERM FUTURE
The final card of the spread represents the likely long-term outcome of the situation, forecasting what may happen over the next six to twelve months.

THE CELTIC CROSS – ISSUES

1 Person in question

2 Possibilities or problems

3 Best course of action

4 Influences from the past

5 Current atmosphere

6 Short-term future

7 Present state of the situation

8 Outside influences

9 Home environment

10 The querent's subconscious feelings

11 Long-term future

A sample reading of the Celtic Cross

This is an example of a reading using the Celtic Cross spread for a female querent. The querent has shuffled the cards while concentrating on the specific question that she is seeking guidance on. The reader has laid out the cards in the Celtic Cross spread and the following interpretation has been made.

Above: Use the Celtic Cross spread to give a Tarot reading in situations when the querent has a specific question that requires a "yes" or "no" answer.

DEATH

1 PERSON IN QUESTION

Meaning: This woman has a whole new outlook on her life, and has discovered new energy both mentally and physically.

FIVE OF
SWORDS

2 POSSIBILITIES OR PROBLEMS

Meaning: She may feel the need to prove herself morally in the right, or to show that she is correct to have her new energetic feelings.

TWO OF
PENTACLES

4 PAST INFLUENCE

Meaning: The situation she is dealing with is one she has been unable to resolve for some time. It is an old and current problem.

KING
OF CUPS

3 BEST COURSE OF ACTION

Meaning: Advice and assistance will come from a very charming and caring man. His response to the issue may well be intuitive as he will be on familiar terms with her.

THE
HERMIT

5 CURRENT ATMOSPHERE

Meaning: Now she should take some "time out" for herself to gather together all her thoughts and feelings and make the decisions that will be right for her.

6 SHORT-TERM FUTURE

Meaning: Over the course of the next three months, this woman will be making an emotional departure from her old lifestyle and going in a new direction.

EIGHT OF CUPS

7 THE PRESENT STATE OF THE SITUATION

Meaning: She will be very popular and sought after as she moves in her new direction.

PAGE OF CUPS

8 OUTSIDE INFLUENCES

Meaning: It would be best to keep her thoughts about her future direction, right or wrong, to herself, so that she can maintain some control.

FOUR OF SWORDS

9 HOME ENVIRONMENT

Meaning: The woman is looking at her present home as a past-tense situation. A new home is likely in the near future.

SIX OF CUPS

Above: After the querent has shuffled the cards, take them back and carefully lay them out in the correct order.

10 SUBCONSCIOUS FEELINGS

Meaning: Subconsciously she feels in a bit of a rut and is looking forward to making even bigger changes when the time is right.

HANGED MAN

11 LONG-TERM FUTURE

Meaning: The woman is right to trust her instincts and gut feelings about life. It is by following her intuition that she has been able to make the choices that she is now acting upon.

HIGH PRIESTESS

The Romany spread

In the past, this spread was widely used by travelling fortune-tellers. It is also known as the Gypsy spread. Today many Tarot readers find it useful because it can look at a person's past, present and future together, thus giving them a more in-depth and overall picture.

The Romany spread is one of the easiest spreads to lay out, and is an effective spread to use when you want to find out what is generally going on in the querent's life, rather than looking for a definite answer to a particular question as in the Celtic Cross spread. It is best used when the querent has various issues that they are dealing with and they want to see how these things will pan out in the future. The querent is simply seeking some general insights into their current situation.

Above: The Romany spread is simple to learn, and gives a good general idea of what is happening in a querent's life.

The Romany spread is an effective tool for getting to the core of an issue which may be hiding under the surface of the querent's subconscious. The querent may not realize the real issues that are troubling them. For example, they may ask about future career aspects when what may actually come up in the cards is personal relationships. This can be ascertained by taking a look firstly at column D, for it is here that the reader can pinpoint the core subject or issues that are affecting the querent at the time of the reading.

Whatever the reader sees in the cards, full one-to-one discussion will help to air the relevant issues at hand.

Above: The Romany spread, also known as the Gypsy spread, was traditionally used by travellers.

The Romany spread explained

The Romany Spread consists of three rows of seven cards, corresponding to the past, present and future. The middle card of each row forms a separate vertical column, and relates to the querent. Begin reading with Column D, then read the rows A, B, and C from left to right.

COLUMN D PINPOINTING THE PERSON

ROW A
THE PAST

1 2 3 4 5 6 7

ROW B
THE PRESENT

8 9 10 11 12 13 14

ROW C
THE FUTURE

15 16 17 18 19 20 21

ROW A THE PAST

The first set of seven cards deals with the querent's past. Cards 1, 2 and 3 represent the more distant past whilst cards 5, 6 and 7 represent the more recent past.

ROW B THE PRESENT

The second set of seven cards engages with present-time issues that are going on for the querent: "What is going on right now?"

ROW C THE FUTURE

The final set of seven cards looks to the future and what is likely to take place. The future is taken to mean a period of the next eight months.

COLUMN D PINPOINTING THE PERSON

Cards 4, 11 and 18 form a central vertical column. This small group of three cards tells us what the querent is really concerned about.

A sample Romany reading for a male

COLUMN D PINPOINTING THE PERSON

By looking first at column D (cards in positions 4, 11 and 18) you can deduce that this man is feeling emotionally balanced with a positive and focused attitude. There is also a nurturing and caring woman in his life.

ROW A THE PAST

In the past, some information about a financial issue (possibly his career) led this man in a new direction, moving away from his childhood and past. This direction, which gave him great excitement, became his way of life. Now he needs to put his trust in a new direction.

ROW B THE PRESENT

As the querent has balance in his home life, he can take on new routines and improve his present situation. This can be best accomplished by being careful with finances and staying well organized.

ROW C THE FUTURE

A blessing in disguise will take place for this man, but it means that a three-way emotional involvement will not work out. He should focus on the friendship of the strong, nurturing female in his life and make the association a firm partnership. By doing so, he will be able to achieve his creative endeavours.

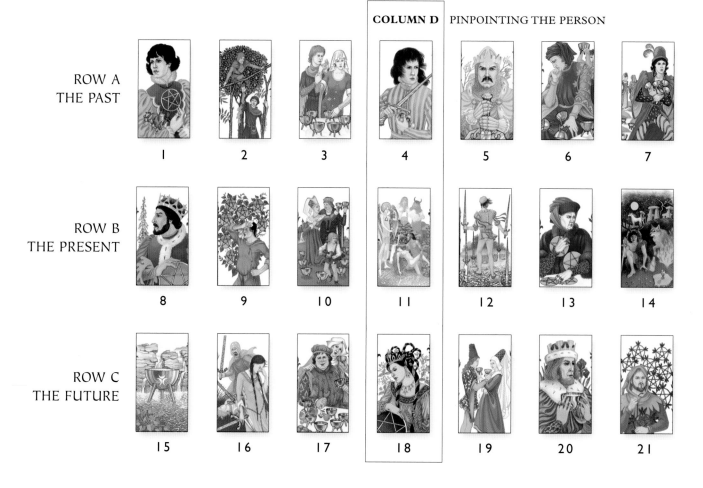

COLUMN D PINPOINTING THE PERSON

ROW A
THE PAST

1   2   3   4   5   6   7

ROW B
THE PRESENT

8   9   10   11   12   13   14

ROW C
THE FUTURE

15   16   17   18   19   20   21

A sample Romany reading for a female

COLUMN D PINPOINTING THE PERSON

By looking first at column D (cards in positions 4, 11 and 18), you can deduce that this woman has some specific goals relating to her career. She is looking for more money and opportunities to support her interests.

ROW A THE PAST

This woman has high moral standards and was stressed in the past due to her sense of fair play. Recently, she has embarked on a particular professional goal by taking new steps and a calculated risk at her own expense, leaving her feeling a bit isolated, like The Hermit.

ROW B THE PRESENT

She is seeking professional advice about her situation, as she feels betrayed professionally by someone, or something has jeopardized her plans. She seems to have the support of a relaxed and philosophical partner who encourages her to make positive choices.

ROW C THE FUTURE

This woman will soon receive some news about a professional goal which will turn fate around in a positive direction, leaving her feeling more emotionally balanced. The final outcome is one of total success in all areas of her life.

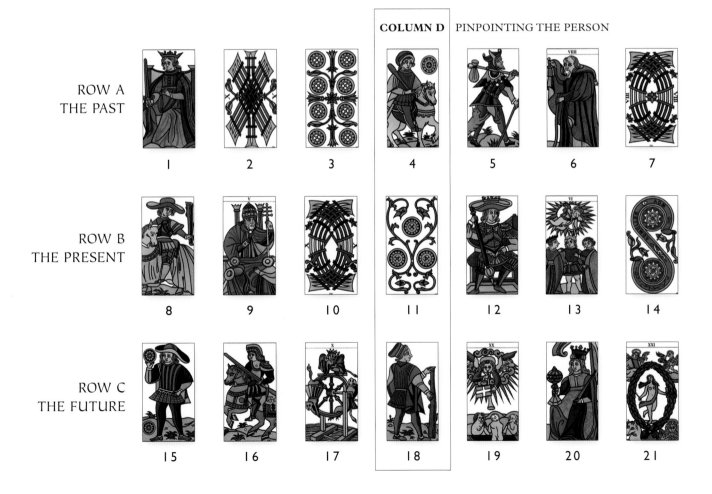

COLUMN D PINPOINTING THE PERSON

ROW A
THE PAST

ROW B
THE PRESENT

ROW C
THE FUTURE

1   2   3   4   5   6   7

8   9   10   11   12   13   14

15   16   17   18   19   20   21

The Tree of Life spread

The Tree of Life spread is very useful for when someone is at a crossroads in life or if they want to know whether they are following the right path in life. The Tree of Life also works effectively as a self-analysis spread. This spread looks more deeply into a person's emotional and spiritual being and helps to pinpoint the core character of an individual. The cards are laid out in rows, which refer to the issues listed below.

> Column F: 1, 3, 7, 13, 21 The Querent
> Row A: Spiritual Goal
> Row B: The Spiritual Plane
> Row C: The Mental Plane
> Row D: The Emotional Plane
> Row E: The Physical Plane

The Tree of Life spread is read firstly by looking deeply into Column F – the querent's character. Then read downwards starting from the top at Row A and finish on Row E.

COLUMN F THE QUERENT
This selection of cards relates to the individual's basic core character personality. It can also be reflective of what the querent is dealing with in their day-to-day lives at the time of the reading. Pay special attention to the number 7 card in Row C as this summarizes the querent's character.

ROW A SPIRITUAL GOAL
This card reflects what the querent would like to achieve spiritually within their life.

Above: The Tree of Life spread is a good spread to use for self-analysis, as well as for Tarot readings for other people. It deals with emotional and spiritual matters.

ROW B THE SPIRITUAL PLANE
Cards 2, 3 and 4 are read together and indicate where the querent is on their spiritual path in life at the time of the reading.

ROW C THE MENTAL PLANE
Cards 5, 6, 7, 8 and 9 are read together and indicate what is in the querent's mind. They can specify any practical issues that they are dealing with which might need some conscious thought at the time of the Tarot reading.

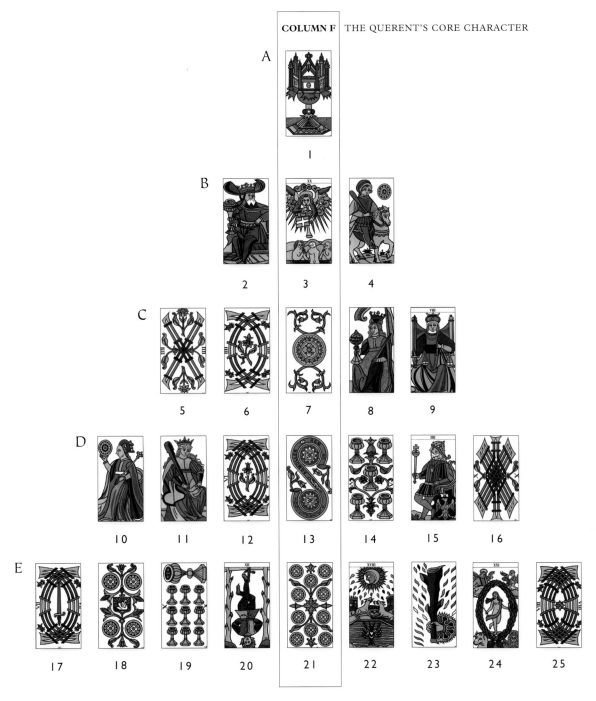

COLUMN F THE QUERENT'S CORE CHARACTER

A   1

B   2   3   4

C   5   6   7   8   9

D   10   11   12   13   14   15   16

E   17   18   19   20   21   22   23   24   25

COLUMN F

ROW D THE EMOTIONAL PLANE

Cards 10, 11, 12, 13, 14, 15 and 16 are read together. This row indicates the emotional or romantic issues the querent is dealing with at the time of the reading.

ROW E THE PHYSICAL PLANE

Cards 17, 18, 19, 20, 21, 22, 23, 24 and 25 are read together and indicate the physical events or issues that may be taking place presently and over the next three months, such as a job promotion, house move or a trip or holiday.

A sample Tree of Life reading for a male

COLUMN F THE QUERENT

By looking first at Column F (Cards 1, 3, 7, 13, 21) you can deduce that this man wants to celebrate life and is always looking to follow a dream. He works creatively and perhaps earns his money through a creative skill or talent.

ROW A SPIRITUAL GOAL

This man is always on the lookout to spiritually invest in more knowledge about himself and is willing to take the time to look at deeper issues of life.

ROW B THE SPIRITUAL PLANE

It appears that he is content with himself and that also he may be someone others seek out for advice on spiritual matters. This man is finding his own enlightenment by working creatively now.

ROW C THE MENTAL PLANE

He is experiencing a high level of success and wishes to develop it further by taking it to a new level, in which he feels he will succeed.

ROW D THE EMOTIONAL PLANE

Things are developing nicely now, but he is feeling defensive about the new changes and is worried that too many unfamiliar faces involved with this recent development could mean a loss of his own desires.

ROW E THE PHYSICAL PLANE

New developments will be received well by others, as will his good reputation. There will be an unforeseen disruptive element that occurs and the necessity for him to let go of a friendship that proves to be untrustworthy. There will be new alliances that will be very secure and help him reach his dreams.

A

B

C

D

E

COLUMN F

A sample Tree of Life reading for a female

COLUMN F THE QUERENT

By looking first at Column F (Cards 1, 3, 7, 13, 21), you can deduce that this woman is a positive thinker and has a balanced outlook to her life and to the world in general. She will always will follow her own path in life.

ROW A SPIRITUAL GOAL

This woman feels spiritually balanced and is not in need of any further spiritual advancement.

ROW B THE SPIRITUAL PLANE

She is seeking spiritually to give to others at this moment in time.

ROW C THE MENTAL PLANE

Very recently she has gained a great energy and passion to give back to others, as she has been given to. She is feeling generous and secure in her own mind.

ROW D THE EMOTIONAL PLANE

This woman is feeling very emotionally creative at this time and feels concerned that her recent acts of generosity may be taken advantage of in some way. She also feels worried about trusting in the feeling of being fulfilled and successful. She is scared that this feeling will not be long-lasting.

ROW E THE PHYSICAL PLANE

There will be a change of events or circumstances in a personal relationship which may cause this woman to choose to walk away from that relationship for a certain period of time. She will focus further on her own personal goals and will not take on any of the stresses of the other person. When the situation balances out to its previous state again, she will return to the relationship with ease once more.

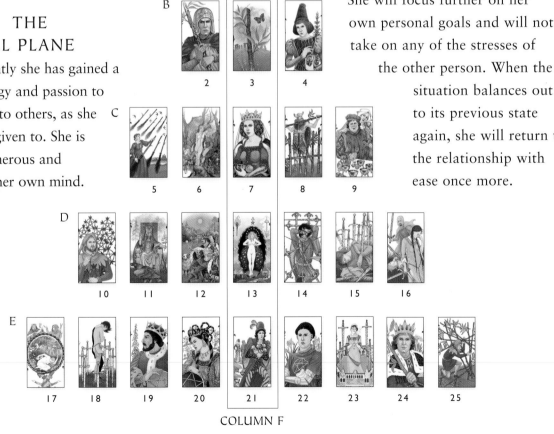

COLUMN F

A final word

Hopefully this book will have touched on some of your more burning questions about the Tarot and answered them. Perhaps it has increased your interest to go on and learn more about this fascinating subject, which has been one of the most well-known forms of personal divination for centuries.

The Tarot is a user-friendly form of divination because of the highly visual prompts that each of the 78 cards contains. The mystery surrounding these almost timeless images stems from their enigmatic and historical past. Brightly-coloured jesters dancing in the sunlight, magicians, priestesses, emperors, kings and queens all meld together to form characters in a vast play. The Tarot has been developed over time into a tool that uses the inherent archetypes and analogies found within these images to tell a story in its own right. It continues a tradition that humans have practised for thousands of years, even before the inception of the Tarot cards themselves.

The art of communication through the use of creative thought, storytelling and the Tarot is one of the greatest tools for continuing that art. By interpreting the Tarot's definitions with discretion and kindness for friends and family, you can continue this age-old practice of learning from the spoken word and picture.

The Tarot can be developed further as a tool by taking one card at a time and meditating

Above: As a beginner, there is a lot to learn about the Tarot, but you will find it a fulfilling and interesting task.

on its symbolic illustration and then noting the thoughts and feelings that it evokes. This method can be used if you are dealing with a specific issue or purely as an exercise to enhance your own self-awareness. You can then try cross-referencing your discoveries with the card definition and see how they tally up.

If it is a specific issue that you are meditating on, perhaps the card definition will link in and help give you an answer to the question. In this way, you can build upon not only the historical and allegorical symbolism of the cards but also the knowledge of the interpretation.

Left: Take time to get to know the individual Tarot cards.

Let the subconscious long-term memory absorb the information and stamp it with your own individual, contemporary experience. This can be done as many times with as many decks of cards as you like. A useful thing to do whilst working through the deck like this is to keep a notebook which could contain your thoughts and ideas about the Tarot cards, plus sample practice readings done for oneself or others. This will also help fix the card definitions in the long-term memory, and provide a good source of reference material to look back on while continuing the study of the Tarot cards.

Left: Keeping a note of your thoughts and feelings while using the Tarot cards will help you build up a reference guide.

Another process that further develops the understanding and learning of the Tarot is exploring its links with astrology. The connections between astrology and Tarot are complex, and although it may take some time to understand them, it is well worth it, because knowing the astrology sign of the person you are reading for and the other people that appear within a spread can help you to quickly and generally group and stereotype them astrologically. This will help in giving you, the reader, a good general background and understanding of the people involved within a situation or issue.

The best time for studying and practising the Tarot is within a peaceful, relaxing atmosphere. The cards are generally a little larger than normal playing cards and can easily be laid out more or less anywhere that has a flat surface and where it is comfortable. This could be sitting on the floor in the lounge or relaxing in natural surroundings outside, or even perhaps sitting on a cosy bed. The most important thing is to make sure that the reader and the querent are relaxed and will not be disturbed.

Remember that the Tarot does not control fate or tell people how to live their lives. It can aid in discussing the options and issues at a given time, providing a clearer picture of a situation or circumstance, but ultimately a person's destiny lies in their own hands. The Tarot is there to be enjoyed for its lively communication, its honesty and its vision. Some believe that it has the ability to heal through the pure and simple fact that someone, the reader, cares enough to listen and advise.

When giving or receiving a reading, the best way of looking at this enigmatic deck of cards is that it is like listening to one's own inner mind or going to a good friend for advice. So please enjoy what you have learned from this book, use it wisely, humanely and with discretion and above all, have fun.

Above: Studying the Tarot should be done in a calm, peaceful environment, so that you feel relaxed.

Index

Acknowledgements
*The authors would like to thank their
students in the study of the Tarot: past,
present and future. Through working
with them over the years, the authors have
evolved their own interests and further
learning on this fascinating subject.*

*The publisher would like to thank the
following individuals and agencies for
loaning items for photography and for
reproducing images: The Astrology Shop,
78 Neal St, London WC2H 9PA; Diane
Flint for the loan of the pewter chalice
(0208 809 0059 for commissions);
Way Out There and Back for Tarot
decks (01903 722666); Mysteries Ltd,
9–11 Monmouth St, London WC2H 9DA.
Picture credits: Bridgeman Art Library
10b, 12t; The Art Archive 10t, 11t; Corbis
11b; Istockphoto 58b, 86b. Illustrations
from the Native American, Gendron,
Pierpont Morgan Visconti-Sforza and
Tarot of Marseilles Tarot decks reproduced
by permission of U.S. Games Systems,
Inc., Stamford, CT 06902 USA.
Copyrights respectively © 1983, 1997,
1985 and 1996 by U.S. Games Systems,
Inc. Further reproduction prohibited.
Illustrations from the IJJ Swiss Tarot
Cards and Tarot of the Old Path
reproduced by permission of the company
© AGM Müller Urania, Switzerland.
Further reproduction prohibited.*